SECRET CREEK

SECRET CREEK

Friendships, pheromones and fly-fishing

Paul Miller

SECRET CREEK
by Paul Miller

Illustrated by Glen Preece

First published in Australia in 2011 by Creek of Peace
PO Box 537
Paddington
New South Wales 2021
Australia

www.creekofpeace.com.au

Paul Miller website www.paulmiller.com.au
Glen Preece website www.glenpreece.com.au

National Library of Australia Cataloguing-in-Publication Data:
Author: Miller, Paul, 1958-
Title: Secret creek: friendships, pheromones and fly-fishing / author: Paul Miller;
illustrator: Glen Preece; editor Peter Gibson.
Edition: 1st American paperback edition 2012
ISBN: 9780975226254
Subjects: Fly fishing – Australia. Fly fishing – New Zealand.
Other Authors/Contributors: Preece, Glen, 1957- , Gibson, Peter, 1957- .
Dewey Number: 799.1240994

Edited by Peter Gibson
Designed by Creek of Peace
Photography by MKImages
Printed in USA by Createspace

Secret Creek is dedicated to
Arthur Frederick Miller,
a consummate fisherman who passed down
the fishing gene to his grandsons Paul and Bruce.
We are forever grateful.

Contents

ACKNOWLEDGMENTS

Secret Creek evolved in part because of a chance meeting with David Smith, editor of the Southern Highlands lifestyle magazine *Highlife*. I cheekily suggested that he needed a regular column on fly-fishing to enhance his magazine. Rather than tossing me out the door, David gave me the go-ahead and encouraged me to write for six years, and for this I am very grateful.

Glen Preece, as you will discover in reading *Secret Creek*, has been a pivotal influence in my fly-fishing life. This book is greatly enhanced by his considerable artistic talent. He is a very skilful angler and I believe one of Australia's most talented artists. His pencil sketches and book cover photograph perfectly illustrate the beauty of fly-fishing and really bring to life so many parts of this book. They say a picture paints a thousand words but I think in Glen's case it is so much more than that.

Peter Gibson of Creek of Peace has been hugely helpful, encouraging a first time author to get a message across, and then bringing *Secret Creek* into being. His professionalism and ability to get the job done meant the process was made so much easier and the end result is a lifelong ambition achieved for me and another friendship in fly-fishing forged.

Dr Rob Sloane, editor of *FlyLife*, the outstanding Australian fly-fishing magazine, was very generous with his advice and encouragement along the way to completing this book.

A huge thank you to my father Geoffrey and stepmother Joan, my brother Justin, my wife Julia and daughter Katie. They have all scratched their heads at one time or another in wonder that a reasonably sane human being could be so fascinated with cold, clear running water and such a seemingly complicated way of fishing. Only people who know the need to be out in the wild on the edge of a stream or on a sand flat peering impatiently and expectantly into the water will understand the incredible pull that fly-fishing exerts. My cousin Bruce, who readers will meet in this book, understands this concept perfectly. How fortunate I am to have a cousin with that level of understanding.

Last, but by no means least, I would like to thank all my special fly-fishing friends who have contributed so much to my enjoyment by sharing their valuable time, friendship and humour. *Secret Creek* is my chance to give something back to this sport that has given me so much enjoyment over the years and which continues to be such an important part of my life.

INTRODUCTION

So many of our family friends and acquaintances ask me what it is about fly-fishing that is so captivating. I will feel very gratified if they and other potential fly-fishers find the answers they are looking for in *Secret Creek*.

If they are sufficiently moved to try fly-fishing, that will be even more rewarding because I know they will discover the lifelong learning curve and tremendous sense of satisfaction that fishing with a fly provides.

They will certainly be captivated by the splendid environment in which they fish, and the friendships they make on their unique journey will be a very special part of the whole experience. They will learn to respect and conserve their quarry and so perpetuate this fascinating sport for the benefit of future generations.

Paul Miller

FIRST TIME ON THE FLY

Some things in life really get the heart pounding, the muscles tensed and the blood coursing through the veins. There are moments of sheer excitement in many varied pursuits and, for a fisherman, catching your first fish on the fly certainly rates up there with the best of them.

Catching that first fish may not need the extraordinary physical training and mental preparation needed to run a marathon. Lifting the rod to set the hook hardly needs the courage of parachutists as they commit to their first jump. In fact many people would think that catching a fish is no huge deal until they realise what a challenge fly-fishing can be for a beginner. The level of knowledge and casting skill that must be put into practice before success becomes a serious possibility makes fly-fishing the pinnacle of piscatorial pursuits.

That first fish can take a long time to get connected. I have heard of people sticking with it for a year or more: it takes patience and persistence. Many a streamside kilometre may be covered over several trips before the magic moment when everything comes together. Hours and hours spent stalking and observing fish will only pay off when you have the ability to put the fly in the right spot and not scare the fish. Get it right and the next few seconds are unbelievably exciting.

Your careful cast lands the fly in a natural manner on the surface of the water. The fish sees your fly and moves towards it. His momentary examination will have your nerves tingling and your heart pounding. Will he take it, will he take it? Come on fish…come on! His whole body is poised to take the fly, he hangs suspended as he surveys the tiny piece of fur and feather almost on the tip of his nose…the suspense is unbearable and it's only been a couple of seconds. Suddenly there is a slight tremor through his body and the decision is made. His fins move and he opens his mouth to gently inhale the fly.

This is make or break time. This is when so many newcomers strike too soon or just lose their nerve altogether. This is the precious moment that all fly-fishers dream about. Success or failure becomes a matter of timing the strike. This simple motion is what often causes beginners to miss their first fish time and time again. This is character building stuff. Having put such a lot of physical and emotional effort into catching their first fish, some people simply give up if they don't succeed early on. They can't seem to cope with the frustration. Sometimes they are just not patient or determined enough. They need to realise in fly-fishing, as in life, persistence is a vital ingredient of success.

Getting that first hook-up is a truly special moment. You have done what you set out to achieve: fooled the fish at its own game. Now the fun really begins as you find yourself attached to a very surprised and frisky fish hell-bent on regaining its freedom. The size of the fish and the terrain in which you have hooked it all have a bearing on your chances of a successful landing. The action is invariably fast and furious and the potential for losing the fish for the inexperienced angler is very much in the fish's favour.

With the line leaving the reel at a rapid rate, the drag on the reel screaming and the rod vibrating and bent precariously, the fish seems in charge. First timers find themselves in sensory overload, but to land this fish successfully requires a cool head—and a bit of luck. Any number of things can go wrong during the course of the tussle and—like Murphy's Law—if it can go wrong it often will. A poorly tied knot may let go. An unseen obstacle may cut the line. The fish may simply be too strong and get into an underwater snag and break off. The angler may panic and put too much pressure on while the fish is still fresh and full of fight. The list goes on and on, sometimes one wonders how a newcomer ever gets their first fish on the bank. It seems like a miracle, and in many ways it is. That is what makes that first fish so special.

Some first time fly-fishers do a very lengthy apprenticeship indeed. Some get their first fish a little sooner. Some do it on their own, while others enlist the help of an experienced friend or professional guide. No matter how you go about catching that first fish, the feeling is the same. Anyone fortunate enough to be present for a friend's first fish will never forget the experience. The sheer excitement of the fight and the look of delight on their face makes any amount of coaching and cajoling worthwhile. The whole exercise can be as nerve-racking for the friend as it is for the first-timer.

I had the honour of helping a new friend, Hugh Seaton, get his first trout a few years ago. Not only was it his first trout on the fly, it was his first ever trout. The whole experience was made all the more interesting because I assumed he was an experienced fly-fisherman and took him to a tricky little secret creek where the fish are quite large and spooky and the casting rather difficult because of the overhanging willows and prolific bank-side blackberry bushes. I thought he would enjoy the added challenge.

As we rigged up our rods, Hugh made it clear that he was new to the game and this put the whole day into an entirely different perspective. Hugh is an anaesthetist by profession and a highly intelligent guy. He is a great listener and really quick on the uptake. I must say from the outset I was very nervous indeed. All of a sudden I had an insight into what professional guides must feel when their clients turn up immaculately attired and equipped, but with little or no experience. I wondered could we work together as a team in the difficult surrounds and get Hugh to hook and land his first trout, on his first trip. Not me hooking the fish and quickly handing over the rod, but Hugh getting it himself. Any experienced angler would know what I mean. I like a challenge, so with me doing my very best to sound confident and casual we set off to do the nearly impossible.

We spent a fascinating day together observing trout cruising and learning how to cast and how to strike when the trout accepted the fly. I caught a couple of nice brown trout early in the day that we spotted together and this gave Hugh an idea of how the whole process works, from the stalk and observation to the careful placement of the dry fly, then the strike and playing out and releasing the fish.

As the day unfolded Hugh's casting improved and he missed several fish by striking too soon or too late, but to his credit he was getting the fly to the fish and fooling them into accepting them. This was a remarkable feat in itself.

Just as the evening light was fading a nice trout rose and took an insect from the surface of a really picturesque pool. It then started to rise repeatedly as it did a beat up and down the pool. Hugh crept forward and did everything right and the magic moment was upon him. He had fooled the trout and connected perfectly. All hell broke loose and the battle was on. Hugh kept the pressure on and followed the brownie up and down the pool and kept him away from one particularly nasty snag where I'd lost a couple of fish over the years. I slid into the creek and netted his trophy. The look on Hugh's face as he held that precious fish was almost beyond description.

A quick photograph in the rapidly diminishing light and Hugh released his first fish to taunt and test us another day. What an achievement on his first day, and what a relief for me. Hugh has since become a very competent fly-fisherman and particularly good friend. Always looking for new challenges Hugh is now experimenting with spey-casting with a lovely rod he built up himself from a Sage kit sourced from the USA. That first trout obviously inspired him enormously, and while he hooked it several years ago, it is pretty clear who is now the one still hooked!

Chapter 2

POETRY IN MOTION

I'm often surprised at just how many people ask what it is about fly-fishing that makes it so different to other forms of fishing and so engrossing as a sport. I guess they are wondering why otherwise rational and intelligent men and women get so deeply interested and involved, and find themselves fishing no other way. There is of course no easy answer. In fact such a question opens up a veritable Pandora's Box of questions. While fly-fishing is obviously a method of fishing, it is the whole process that makes it charming, absorbing and both physically and intellectually stimulating. One special fly-fishing friend of mine, Ann Lee, is a very sprightly lady in her early seventies. When asked this question recently on a winter trip to New Zealand, where she kept most of the guys honest, she simply said it is everything about fly-fishing that she likes—the whole picture, the whole package.

So what makes up this whole package? One answer that immediately comes to mind is the places fly-fishers go to fish. The diverse environments, the incredible beauty and contrasts between fresh and saltwater locations, snow clad alpine scenery to tropical sand flats with clean sand, warm blue water and distant coral reefs. Of course you can fish these environs with bait or lures and still enjoy yourself and catch fish, so this suggests to me at least that it must be the method rather than the location.

From a physical point of view I've always preferred the fight any fish gives on a long fly rod when compared to a shorter spinning rod—something to do with leverage and the longer rod seeming to have less of that. Less leverage means a fairer contest between man and fish, and a greater feeling of connectedness—if there is such a word. Bait fishing is a great way to get a feed but waiting around for a fish to bite is a bit too slow for me. Casting a spinning rod and lures accurately requires great skill but you only make one cast at a time, and the casting process relies on the weight of the bait and sinker or lure to pull the line off the reel. You can sometimes find yourself feeling a little heavy handed when the sinker and bait hurtle noisily into the surf.

The exact opposite is true for fly-casting. Putting it really simply, the weight of the tapered fly line in combination with the act of casting bends the rod and allows the angler to extend the line and continue casting until he or she is ready to present the virtually weightless fly gently onto the water. This is an important part of the beauty of fly-fishing—the constant casting action involved and to some extent the degree of difficulty and finesse involved in presenting the fly in such a manner as to not frighten the fish. There are times when a more aggressive casting approach pays dividends, like in heavy winds or when large insects are being blown onto the water, but generally a gentle delivery wins the day.

Working your way up a stream, and expertly extending your cast to drop your fly delicately in likely looking spots, keeps you on the move and very much involved in the whole environment around you. Presenting a fly to a fish you can see in either fresh or saltwater is the ultimate thrill and requires quick, accurate casting and considerable finesse. I'm certain that this is one of the major attractions to anglers fishing with the fly. It certainly is for me. Sneaking up on a fish without it seeing you and being able to watch it in its natural environment is a real buzz. Being able to fool it with a fly and feeling that sense of connection is something special.

When we see fly-casting portrayed in television commercials or fishing programs it looks so relaxed and easy. The angler seems to effortlessly move the rod backwards and forwards and the line follows in long languid loops. The whole image is of grace and style. It is the application of subtle power that creates this graceful method of delivering a fly to the target, and this feeling of finesse is in itself so appealing in a physical sense. Some people get the feel and others do not. I guess it's a bit like some people having a musical ear and others not. For people with a love of fly-fishing and a natural sense of rhythm and timing there is nothing more rewarding or perhaps sensuous than the feel of a good cast. Famous American fly-fisher Mel Krieger talked about 'poets' and 'engineers' when he compared and broadly categorised the two types of learners he encountered in his casting schools. The engineers had to have casting explained to them in ways they could understand. The poets didn't need much scientific explanation; they just needed to be shown how to 'feel' the cast. Mel Krieger was a very amusing man, and I think he rather fancied himself in the poets group, but his message was: there is no single right way to learn casting. People from all walks of life and vocation can become excellent fly-casters. Engineers and poets can have just as much fun and success and enjoy the delights of casting in their own special ways.

In the beginning, learning to cast is for many people both frustrating and hilarious. They assume because it looks easy, that it is. They are often in for a shock. A really competent angler makes fly-casting look easy, but as in life, anything that someone can make look easy is invariably difficult, and takes some time to master. To learn the art of fly-casting is to learn patience and timing. For some people it goes way beyond that and becomes an end in itself. Some people get into competitive casting and rarely fish, while others satisfy themselves with developing their skills on stream or lake, and competition with others or themselves is the furthest thing from their minds.

When a beginner first picks up a fly rod and tries to make a cast they invariably pull some fly line from the reel and flail away until the line falls unceremoniously in a tangle on their head. Depending on the individual's personality and sense of humour, this can be very funny or the end of their fly-fishing career. If they are doing this on their own it will decide just how keen they are to persevere. With a competent friend or instructor it will be just the beginning and with some help and advice they will find themselves having a great time learning the basics of fly-casting. They need to learn to smoothly lift the bulk of the fly line off the water then flick it up and back, then pause with their rod just beyond vertical to allow the line to straighten out behind them. Then, and only then, can they apply power to the forward cast to get the line moving forward to present the fly or to continue false casting. It sounds easy but it takes quite a while to get it all together. It is just a matter of timing and trial and error.

Beyond the basics there is a world of techniques that can be learnt and utilised in the seemingly endless number of situations that fly-fishing offers us. This is also part of the charm of fly-fishing in that the learning curve is never ending. Some sports like tennis or football are very physical and see your sporting career end at a relatively early age. Fly-fishing and fly-casting do not require youth and sheer physical strength, but rather technique and timing. Many ladies around the world are successful fly-casters because they listen and willingly accept quality instruction—they realise that fly-casting is about subtlety rather than strength. Some of the world's finest fly-casters are in their senior years and that should give us all great encouragement—we can now look forward to getting older, and better!

To become a competent caster requires balanced equipment and the help of a patient friend or professional instructor. There are excellent books and videos on the subject available from specialist fly-fishing shops. You can join a fly-fishing club and take part in their fly-casting days, participate in club outings to the fresh or saltwater environs and soak up as much knowledge and advice as possible. There are fly-fishing magazines to which you can subscribe, and these are great for reading on rainy days and piling up around the house and beside your bed to generally send your better half insane. Better still, try and get them involved, and see if they get as badly bitten by the fly-fishing bug as you. We've all heard the old saying 'if you can't beat them, join them', but I've never been quite sure in what spirit that should be taken. I guess it is whatever works for you and yours.

Remember the pleasures of fly-casting and fly-fishing are not secret men's business. There are many men out there whose wives, girlfriends or daughters have discovered the joys of fly-casting and fishing, and they often find their ladies literally cast circles around them. With their egos under control, these are very lucky men indeed. Let's face it: the family that fly-fishes together stays together! Well, maybe that's a long bow to draw, but there is no doubt that fly-fishing is a very involving pursuit in so many ways. Good fly-casting is for me, and for so many of my friends, nothing less than poetry in motion.

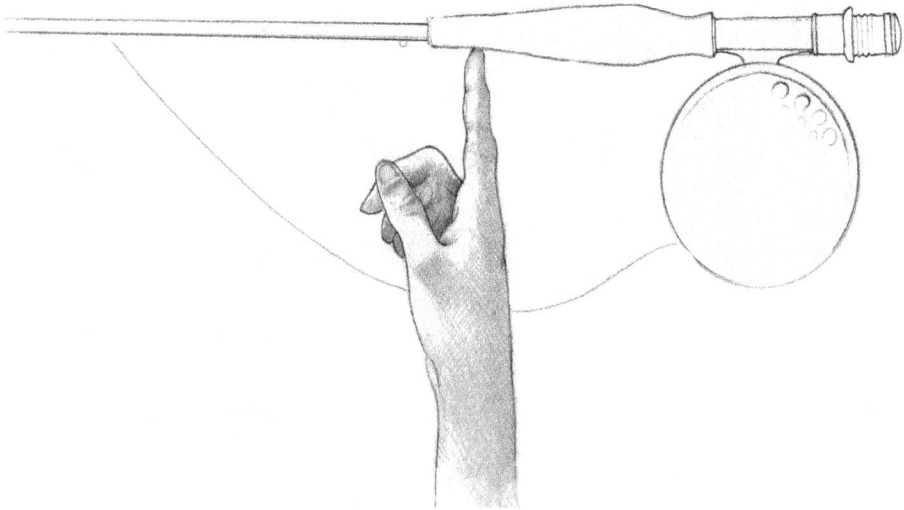

Chapter 3

A BALANCED OUTFIT

One of the most important aspects of fly-fishing for people new to the sport is acquiring an outfit that is correctly balanced and comfortable to cast. It also needs to be suited to what you are trying to catch. There is nothing more discouraging than being sold a rod, reel and line that does not match the job at hand. This makes learning to cast and catch fish almost impossible.

A few years ago I bought a beautiful burgundy coloured seven foot, two piece 3-4 weight Hardy Deluxe fly rod in as new condition with the plastic wrap still protecting the high-grade cork handle. It was an ultra slow action rod and I bought it very reasonably. I also purchased what appeared to be a matching Hardy Featherweight reel loaded with a fluorescent orange floating fly line. The salesperson said the rod had been traded in by a doctor for another rod just the week before. When I spotted the reel in another cabinet he said that it was also part of the trade-in. I took this beautiful outfit home, put it together and was horrified to find it was virtually impossible to cast. I rang the store back the next morning and asked why the good doctor had traded it in. I had my suspicions, and the salesperson confirmed them when he said it was because he couldn't cast it to save himself!

With such a superb rod and reel there could only be one answer: the line. A friend of mine who is technically minded had a book that told us what various line sizes should weigh. We measured the appropriate front thirty feet of line and found it was a 1 weight! No wonder the outfit was traded in. You had to cast the combination to realise just how bad the level of imbalance between line and rod really was. As soon as I put a four-weight double tapered line on the Hardy it changed instantly from well-nigh impossible to a delicious casting tool. Whoever put that outfit together originally for the good doctor either had no idea what they were doing or had a line in an incorrectly marked box. They may have wanted to get even with him for some earlier misdiagnosis! Perhaps he saved their mother-in -law…or something like that! While I felt a bit sorry for the doctor—OK, a very tiny bit sorry—I was really rather glad about the mix up because I would never have had the pleasure of owning such quality equipment otherwise. I used that outfit sparingly on days when I wanted to treat myself or make the tussle a special challenge. I caught several nice trout on it over the years before selling it to a very good friend in a weak moment, but at least he appreciates its balance and pride of ownership. He says he bought it for his three-year-old son and will give it to him when he turns twelve. I would bet a rod of similar value that it will get a fair bit of exercise before the young fellow gets his hands on it! Good luck to him. I hope he grows up a fly-fisherman and appreciates the balance of his Dad's special gift.

When searching for that perfectly balanced outfit I guess the message is that purchasing your gear from a specialist shop with experienced salespeople is a great start, and the old saying that you only get what you pay for is equally true in the gear freak paradise that is fly-fishing. Quality equipment does not come cheaply but it will last a lifetime. It will also repay your initial investment many times over in terms of speeding up the learning process and providing tackle that you will continue to enjoy and grow in to, rather than out of.

In choosing a suitable outfit it helps to understand that the mechanics of fly-casting are the opposite of normal fishing. Most casting, whether it is with bait and sinker, lures or spinners, involves throwing a weight that pulls a fine nylon line off the reel to make the cast. With fly-casting the fly weighs virtually nothing. It is the weight of the thick tapered fly line and the act of casting that loads the rod and delivers the fly to the target. As we false cast and aerialise the line we pull more and more fly line off the reel until we are satisfied with the distance then we make a final presentation cast to deliver the fly gently to the target. With larger salmon flies and saltwater flies tied on large, heavy hooks the principle remains the same but more robust rods and heavier lines are used to cast the heavier flies.

Rods today are given a line rating based on the American Fishing Tackle Manufacturers Association (AFTMA) and this is usually a good guide to what line to buy to match the rod. Most rods have a description printed on them just in front of the cork handle and it might look like this: 'G.Loomis GLX 9' 8wt 4pc', which means the brand of rod, brand or type of graphite used in its construction, length of rod, recommended weight of line and how many pieces it breaks down to for ease of transport. A nine foot eight weight makes an ideal heavy lake rod or good all-round saltwater rod.

Similarly, an old favourite of mine, a 'Sage SP 490-3 Graphite IV' is a 'Smooth Performance' four-weight nine foot, three piece rod made from graphite IV. This is a superb stream rod for trout. Being lighter in construction it throws a lighter line that causes less disturbance when it lands on the water and this means a more delicate delivery of the fly and less chance of spooking the ever-alert trout.

Modern fly lines also come in a large number of line weights from 0 to 15 and in different profiles for different types of casting and fishing situations. They are generally rated on the basis of what the first thirty feet of line actually weighs and this is then related to the strength of rod necessary to load properly with this weight and rebound to cast the line. Some lines float and then there are numerous lines that sink at different speeds. But wait, there's more! Lines also come in a myriad of different colours. If you think this all sounds like a minefield then you are probably right. And yes, there's more! We still need to discuss the incredible range of reels available today!

In the old days you either bought an inexpensive English reel that worked well or an expensive one like the range offered by the House of Hardy that were, and still are superb pieces of engineering. Today there are excellent reels made all around the world. Some feature disc drags for controlling the fish taking line, and many are made of ultra-light space age materials like aluminium and graphite which make them very light indeed. A word of warning here: very light reels often do not balance longer heavier rods and make casting very tiring. A heavier reel balances the outfit better and acts like a counterbalance and relieves the casters wrist and elbow from having to allow for this imbalance. The trend to large arbor reels means we can retrieve line faster and with less line memory. Technology marches onwards and upwards, at least most of the time.

A good rule of thumb when buying an outfit is to mount the reel on the rod and drape the matching line around the reel and see if the rod hangs horizontally when held lightly in the casting hand. If the tip of the rod falls to the floor then the reel is too light. If the tip goes far above horizontal then the reel is too heavy. Getting this balance right makes for a much easier casting outfit and will mean far less fatigue and muscle soreness at the end of the day. A well-balanced outfit actually works for you as opposed to against you.

The manufacturers today usually mark their reels with some sort of numbers to help match them up to the rated rod and line combination. A reel with '45' or '678' suggests they are well suited to the range of lines of those numbers. The smaller reels accommodate the lighter and less bulky lines while the larger reels have more room for backing line and bulkier fly lines for bigger fish and larger flies. There is obviously a vast difference in size and construction between reels designed for trout and marlin fishing.

How does the beginner get through this maze? As suggested earlier the best solution is to go to a specialist shop or get an experienced friend to help you. As you become more knowledgeable you will start to develop your skills and get your own ideas about what balance means to you personally. It is easy to get really technical but many of the very expensive powerful graphite rods are often better suited to one line rating greater than recommended on the rod.

This also depends on whether you are using a weight forward or double taper line. Generally you can overload with a weight forward and use a double taper of the recommended weight or one line size lighter than what it says on the side of the rod.

The reason for this is the weight forward is designed as a shooting line, with a greater proportion of the weight of the line in the relatively short front tapered section. This enables a shorter length to be false cast and then the line is shot forward with the thinner, lighter rear portion of the line following the heavier front or shooting taper to the target.

The double taper on the other hand has the thickest part of the line at the midpoint, tapering equally and gradually to each end. These lines are generally better for presentation casting where distance is less important than delicate presentation. They also have the advantage of being reversible when you have worn out one end. I particularly like double tapers but there has been a growing trend towards weight forward lines in recent years. This is partly because the faster rods we are being offered are meant for casting greater distances when loaded with the weight of a forward tapered line. Of course it comes as no surprise to experienced anglers that these high-tech weapons don't necessarily get us more fish because we can cast further. They can also give us 'caster's elbow' if we are not careful. There are rods for casting and there are rods for fishing and there are combinations of these rods and lines to suit every angler's style and preference.

The principle remains the same however irrespective of line type: a little extra weight assists in bending today's light yet incredibly powerful casting tools, particularly for shorter range casting by beginners and intermediates. Sometimes it pays to overload your fast taper graphite rod by as much as three line sizes if you are fishing small streams or sneaking around lake margins and only making short quick fire casts.

My favourite stream rod is a nine foot four weight Sage that I often fish with a seven-weight line and long leader in exactly these situations. The short length of heavy floating line beyond the rod tip gets the rod working and propels the long leader so well that the fly gets to where I want it with virtually no fly line on the water. This means the trout in my favourite secret creeks see only the fly and perhaps a little leader. Such a set-up allows for quick stealthy presentations and increases the chances of fooling our speckled friends dramatically. Such an outfit is the end result of a lot of experimentation and is well suited to short range work. Get too much fly line out and the rod starts to struggle. It becomes overloaded and can't deliver the fly line, let alone the fly. Horses for courses I guess.

The other benefit of over-weighting I find useful is when teaching friends to cast. A quality rod over-weighted a couple of line sizes smoothes out a beginner's casting and helps them to get the feel of the rod loading and unloading with a short and manageable length of line in the air. Once they have the feel of what a cast should be they can then experiment with lines sizes more closely related to their rod's recommended line size. This is a great trick and can help beginners to pick up fly-casting very quickly.

A few years ago I accepted an invitation from Illawarra Fly Fishers to give a day of casting instruction. I asked them to bring their favourite rods and if possible to bring along a line two sizes heavier than they would normally use on their favourite rod. This club has a lot of very enthusiastic members and many of them are very good casters. They were a bit sceptical of the two-line-weights-heavier approach but very quickly got to feel parts of their cast they had never felt before. When they swapped back to their recommended lines some were happy and others said they actually preferred the feel of the heavier lines. The looks on some of the faces of the best casters, as they explored the differences a couple of line weights can make was most amusing. Guys who were by any standard very good casters, found something new and intriguing in the concept. Looks of scepticism gave way to looks of amazement which then gave way to looks of concentration, as they tried different casts and felt their rods working in ways they had never experienced. It was certainly food for thought and they hopefully took home some new ideas to play with.

The whole point of the exercise for the experienced casters was to challenge long held assumptions about casting, and what is a balanced outfit. For the experienced casters it also gave them something to experiment with in the future. The inexperienced casters said without exception that they found casting easier. I put this down to the heavier line slowing down and dampening their casting. The line also made the rods work more and gave the new casters a real feeling of the various stages of the cast and when to accelerate and when to stop their rods during the casting process. It also helped them feel the right moment for shooting line and helped them form smooth slightly more open loops, which aided the delicacy of their presentations on the casting pond. It was a lot of fun and an eye-opener for all concerned.

When all is said and done, the charm of fly-fishing is largely in the method. People take up fly-fishing and are hooked for life by the hypnotic charm of good fly-casting. The feel of a good fish on a fly rod is quite different to any other method and a truly well balanced quality outfit only serves to heighten the experience.

Chapter 4

CHOOK ON A HOOK

Fur and feathers are the main materials used in traditional fly-tying and one of the most important ingredients for crafting flies is chicken feathers. These feathers are known collectively as a cape and the individual feathers are known as hackles. They are used in numerous ways to represent different parts of the flies we tie, to fool all manner of fish from trout to tuna.

The first reference to fly-fishing and fly-tying is generally acknowledged to come from a book entitled *On the Nature of Animals* published around 200 AD. The author Claudius Aelianus described people fishing in the river Astraeus in Macedonia. It is presumed that the fish were brown trout as they were described as being spotted. It would seem that in those days the Macedonians were fishing with primitive metal hooks covered in red thread and wax coated cock feathers. These are the earliest described fly-fishermen but they may not have been the first.

The next reference to anglers tying flies and fishing for pleasure comes from fifteenth century England. In 1496 Dame Juliana Berners described fishing methods at that time in an article entitled 'A Treatyse of Fysshynge Wyth an Angle' as part of the *Book of St. Albans*. Dame Juliana was apparently the Abbess of a Benedictine nunnery in Sopwell and believed that the proper fisherman had to be an idealist, a philosopher and a nature worshipper. It was her view that fishermen should build their own rods and tie their own flies. To this end she designed twelve fly patterns, one for each month of the year.

While the literature on fly-fishing has burgeoned along with technology since Dame Juliana's time, there are some fundamentals that have not changed in terms of the traditional materials used to replicate insects and the humble chicken feather is still very much a part of fly-tying.

The world's domestic chickens descend from what fly-tyers have long referred to as jungle cocks. These birds still roam the southern jungles of India, and many have unbelievable feathers. From an economic perspective, the most inexpensive capes come from India and the most expensive from America. The reason for this is based on quality and quantity. The Indian capes are readily available from the enormous population of free-range birds but are generally of poor quality. The American capes are at the other extreme in terms of quality and price and there are very good reasons for the increased demand for these capes by enthusiastic fly-tyers around the world.

Beginning in the early 1900s, there has been an increasing demand for quality feathers with individual barbs that are stiff and strong and with stems that are flexible enough to be wound around small hooks. These feathers are what make the fly float upright and the better the quality of the feather the longer a dry fly will float, particularly in a tumbling stream. Cock feathers are usually stiffer than hen feathers and so are more popular for tying dry flies. Hen feathers on the other hand are softer and better suited to wet flies that are fished below the surface as they pulse with the water currents and give life to the flies like few other materials can.

In his extraordinary two-volume set entitled *Fish Flies* American author Terry Hellekson wrote that a small number of poultry producers in America who had a personal interest in tying their own flies started to experiment with selective breeding programs aimed specifically at feather production. This concentration on breeding for feather quality, as opposed to meat or egg production, has produced the extraordinary variety and quality of feathers we have available today. Names like Metz, Hoffman and Whiting are associated with hackles of incredible quality and diversity both in terms of colours and consistency.

Various breeds have been experimented with and chicken fanciers would be well aware of the Plymouth Rock which fly-tyers call the 'grizzly'. The Plymouth Rock was a bird the American poultry industry recognised early on as an all rounder—a bird that could be used for both meat and eggs. On top of this the roosters often produced very good dry fly quality hackle. Unfortunately the demands of a burgeoning population meant that the poultry industry in America developed newer more productive breeds and the Plymouth Rock fell from favour. Fortunately a few smaller farmers stuck with the Plymouth Rock because of its reputation as a multiple purpose bird. Between the late twenties to the mid sixties there was experimentation carried out to develop the perfect feather producing bird and it was Henry Hoffman who found a pair of bantam Plymouth Rocks at the 1966 Pacific International Livestock Exposition in Portland, Oregon. According to Hellekson, Hoffman credits these birds as having saved him ten years in his breeding program and they allowed him to make great genetic strides in such a short time. By the early 1980s his capes were the stuff of legend.

Henry Hoffman only produced 2,200 roosters per year but in 1989 he sold his business to Dr Tom Whiting, a specialist with three degrees including a PhD in poultry management and genetics. Dr Whiting retained the Hoffman name and acquired other breeding stock and began developing other coloured feathers admirably suited to tying flies. Whiting Farms now produce approximately 46,000 roosters per year!

In the mid 1970s another American poultry producer called Buck

Metz was invited by a friend to go fly-fishing and he became hooked on the sport. He started tying his own flies and was reluctant to buy feathers as he obviously had plenty running around his own farm. Through trial and error he and his family bred superb hackled birds and they expanded from meat and egg production into the feather business. Today Metz Hatchery Inc raises around 60,000 birds annually.

What started out as chook on a hook has developed exponentially into an international industry that provides fly tying enthusiasts around the world with the perfect feather, to tie the ultimate fly, to fool all manner of game fish in both fresh and saltwater locations.

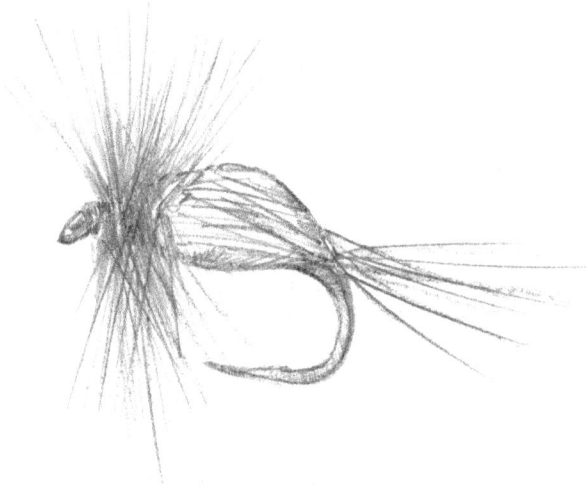

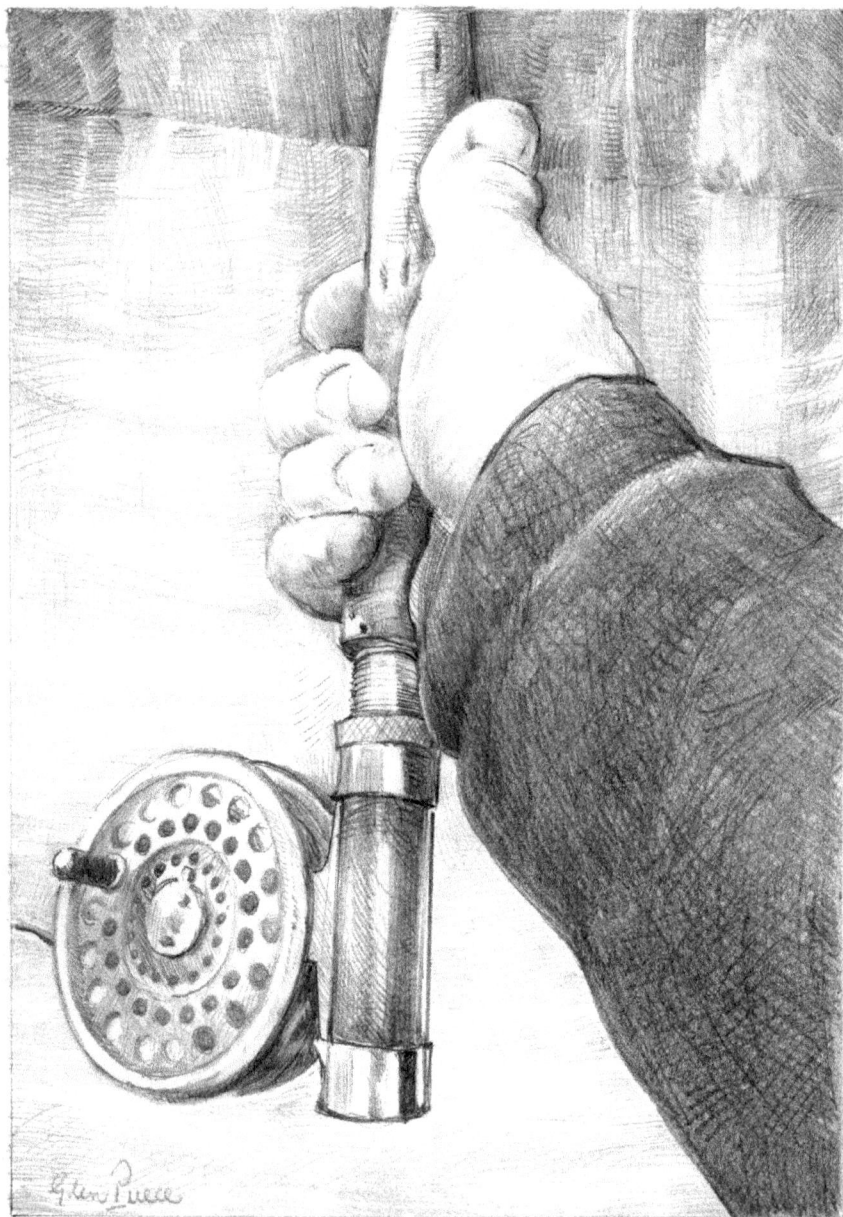

Chapter 5

THE EDUCATED WRIST

Think of any sport and an expert always makes it look easy. This is nowhere better demonstrated than in fly-casting where a good fly-caster makes the whole process of extending a fly line and delivering the fly to the target look both effortless and graceful. I often think of casting as being poetry in motion and one of the most enjoyable facets of fly-fishing, and the most obvious part that differentiates it from other forms of fishing.

To achieve a high level of casting skill takes many years of practice. It reminds me of the story about famous South African golfer Gary Player, who when asked about his incredible career and personal skills, attributed his success with words to the effect, 'It seems the harder I practise the luckier I get!' The same can be said of fly-casting where the more you practice, the more fish you will fool with your increasingly effective presentations.

Of course practice in any sport is only relevant if you are practising the right things. With casting a fly, it is a matter of understanding the basics of the cast and building on those skills as time goes by. It is relatively easy to teach a beginner to cast a fly but it takes a long time and a passion for the sport before a beginner becomes anything like an expert.

One of my favourite (and appropriately surnamed) fly-casting instructors is American Doug Swisher who talks about the 'educated wrist' and how it is vital for successful casting. What Swisher is referring to are the subtle movements of the wrist and the important part these movements play in accelerating and stopping the rod in the casting stroke. A really effective cast involves picking the line off the water and aerialising it by accelerating the rod then stopping it just beyond vertical for a moment to allow the line to unfurl behind, then applying the power again through a combination of casting effort and the rod's flexing action to bring the line back—and deliver the fly to the intended target. Doug calls the part that a flexible wrist plays in the whole casting operation, the 'micro-second wrist'. It is a pretty neat way of saying that the flexing action of the wrist only takes part for a micro-second and that is where the subtlety lies with his method. Doug has a couple of very good videos that illustrate his method as well as another couple on stream-craft and how to cast to all parts of a stream—or as he calls it 'fishing around the clock'. I highly recommend them all.

There is certainly no single way to cast a fly, but this is where the experts differ in their opinions on the perfect casting action. Not only do they differ, but also they seem to do so on a national basis. Many English instructors like to promote a stiff wrist in the casting action and a greater reliance on the casting arm being kept beside the body to achieve a good casting action. This maintains control of the desirable tight loop in the fly line that is created during the cast. In fact I've seen pictures of beginners in English magazines with a scarf tied around their forearm well below their wrist and connected to the base of the rod below the reel to completely inhibit the use of any wrist action. American instructors seem to prefer a much less rigid approach where there is a lot more arm action and the wrist is more flexible and used to accelerate the cast. Americans are also into saltwater fly-fishing in a big way and they tend to use a bit of a javelin approach with their arm reaching out behind them for casting these big flies with very powerful rods and heavy lines. In Australia we seem to be a mix of both and with a few variations of our own. As you might expect, the Aussie larrikin is alive and well in the sometimes starchy world of fly-casting techniques.

Noted Tasmanian professional casting instructor and guide Peter Hayes, seems to advocate an essentially rigid wrist rotated through ninety degrees, a style he has developed for tournament casting where accuracy is everything and where he has enjoyed enormous success. For my own part, I prefer to teach people to cast with a more comfortable grip rather like the way you grip a golf club. I'm a great believer in a flexible wrist for an increasingly competent caster because of the subtlety and finesse that can be introduced to the casting action by the use of an educated wrist.

Fly-casting is after all about finesse. As one learns more about different ways to cast and present a fly the enjoyment of the whole process grows in leaps and bounds with every new technique mastered. With increasing skill also comes the need for less effort to achieve the same results. Really competent casters make it look effortless because it is. Beginners flail away and can't understand why they can't extend the line any distance at all. They assume that they should cast even harder and hurl the rod back and forth as though they were throwing a huge sinker and bait out into the surf. All this energy is wasted because they are actually working against themselves and their fly rod and line. The inevitable and hilarious result is a pile of fly line falling on their head rather than extending out and delivering the fly where they want it.

The trick with fly-casting is to slow everything down and let the rod and line work together as they are designed to do. Far too many new casters try and muscle their rod and this is not at all helpful in making a controlled cast. An educated wrist is an integral part of this process in that you get the line moving slowly as you lift the rod then accelerate to the top of the cast and stop the rod. You allow the line enough time to extend behind you, and only then do you attempt the forward part of the cast by bringing the power on again smoothly to allow the line to fully extend in front of you. If you are false casting, where you are wanting to extend the line between casts and keep the line up in the air, then you stop the rod high on the back-cast and the forward cast, and only drop the rod tip on the forward cast when you've finished the power stroke and want to present the fly .

I had a great deal of fun teaching my friend Martin Nadas to cast a fly on the casting pond I have at my home. We started with a quick talk about the rod, reel and line, and how they all function in fly-fishing. Martin's father had been a really keen fly-fisherman and left all his lovingly maintained and cherished equipment to Martin—how good would that be—to have your father's collection and have the desire to take up where he left off?

We began by getting the back-cast right and then started on the timing. Martin was so excited that he couldn't resist false casting and his timing was completely out. He just couldn't bring himself to hesitate on the back-cast. He was swish-swishing away like fury despite my protests, and you guessed it, the end result was a pile of line on his head and a huge amount of laughter between us. I ended up tricking him by putting a much heavier line on his rod (an eight weight on his six weight) so that it slowed him down and gave him the feel of loading the rod and the feel of the line pulling on the rod tip in the back and forward casts. It took him no time at all to get the feel, and start putting out some reasonable casts. A few weeks later he came on a club trip to New Zealand and caught some excellent trout on big dry flies in some of the superb rivers around Turangi in the middle of the North Island. We couldn't wipe the smile off his face for weeks afterwards!

Early on, Martin asked me whether he should have a rigid wrist and we answered that by letting him try both methods. He found the rigid approach most uncomfortable and very hard on his casting shoulder. The more flexible wrist proved a lot more effective and easier physically. It allowed him to keep his casting elbow nearer his side in the English style, but also gave him better leverage with the rod by keeping his elbow lower. I had to curb his tendency to be too wristy and flicking the power on towards the end of the cast. This just causes overly tight loops and tangles. With a little effort on concentrating, and flexing the rod more slowly and deeply with only a little wrist movement, the loops opened up to a nice controllable width and the casts became easier and more extended.

Casting looks deceptively easy on the television in four-wheel drive and beer commercials. The reality is that almost anyone can become a good caster but it takes both patience and dedication. The serious fly-caster needs to master many techniques. An educated wrist goes a long way towards the goal of every serious fly-caster, to get to a stage where they can actually feel the energy transfer working through the rod. In fly-casting it probably doesn't get any more sensual than that!

Chapter 6

WHICH FLY SHOULD I USE?

When spring is in the air, the new season for the stream fisherman is agonisingly close. In New South Wales the long weekend in October signals the end to those short cold days of winter and never fails to put a smile on the face of any serious fly-fisher. Just the mention of the October long weekend brings back memories of those exciting opening days of seasons past. It's pure pleasure to be out again on the stream with running water and rod and reel in hand, to see how our precious trout have fared over winter. It's not necessarily the best time for catching lots of trout as they recover from winter but it's great to be out there with a new season all before us.

In the Southern Tablelands south of Sydney we have some prime early season stream fishing and it only gets better as the weather warms into November and December. The lakes also start to warm in their upper layers after the extremes of winter and the insect life starts to proliferate. Our local lakes like Pejar and Fitzroy Falls start to see insect activity and this encourages the trout into the lake margins in search of food. Dark wet flies are best early in the season. At this time of the year we fish dark brown, green or black nymphs or woolly worms, slow and deep on a floating or clear intermediate (slow sinking) line.

Why is that? Well let me try and explain. At the heart of fly-fishing is the need to know what techniques and flies to use and when they are appropriate. What trout eat and when is the most fundamental information around which most techniques revolve. While trout feed on a huge variety of aquatic and land living insects, it is the mayfly hatches that are often the highlight of the fly-fisherman's calendar on streams around the world.

Mayflies are of the order ephemeroptera—Latin for 'short lived on the wing'. If something is described as being ephemeral that means it is around for only a very short time. That is something of an understatement for mayflies, as we will see.

Mayflies start their lives as eggs deposited by their mothers into the water. They drift down into the stream bed or aquatic plants and after several weeks they change into tiny nymphs. Over the course of twelve months they grow to maturity and are relatively safe from the trout as they live and cling to the underside of rocks or plants and wait for nature's signal to wriggle up to the surface of the stream where they break through the surface tension of the water and hatch into what are known as duns. They discard their whole body case and put up their wings to dry before they take off, change into their next body phase as spinners, find a partner and mate, then die. The females live for a couple of days and the males are generally only good for one day above water. So they live a year underwater and only a few hours above. Now that's what I call short lived—they have to find a mate and procreate as soon as possible or miss out!

Trout feed on the nymphs of numerous species throughout their life cycles but particularly when they are at their most vulnerable between the stream bottom and the water's surface. If the mayfly survives the trip to the surface and the time it takes to shed its shuck and dry its wings as it floats along on the water surface, it only has one or two chances at mating within a few short hours before it dies and drifts off down the stream as a spent spinner. It really is a wonder that any survive the frenzied feeding of the trout during this tremendously vulnerable time, but mayflies and other similar stream-born insects hatch in such numbers that they are assured of survival and continuation of the species.

Early in our Southern Highlands season there are still some trout, subject to river levels, in the Wollondilly River that feeds the enormous Warragamba Dam. These fish spend most of the year in the cool depths of Warragamba but come up the Wollondilly in winter when the water flows and temperature is right. Over the years there have been some amazing runs, mixed with very sparse or non-existent runs during droughts. Warragamba still acts as a fabulous refuge for both brown and rainbow trout in summer and it is a tremendous shame that anglers are not allowed to fish there by the controlling water authority.

When the trout do run up spawning rivers it is possible to catch them on bright orange trout egg imitation flies, or on flies the colour of the streambed. I've caught beautiful rainbow trout in the Wollondilly on green mudeyes which match perfectly with the larval form of the dragonfly that they copy. These insects live in huge numbers in the rocky sections of this river. Of course you can catch trout year round in higher elevation streams on nymphs by matching the colour of the available nymphs which you can find by simply lifting a rock in the stream and observing the colour of the nymphs holding on underneath the rock.

As the season progresses and we start to see some serious mayfly hatches we continue to imitate parts of the mayfly's life cycle by fishing nymphs whenever there is no sign of surface activity. We use dry flies which float when we can see the mayflies hatching and the trout taking them from the surface. Try small dries like the Royal Wulff, March Brown, Red Tag, or my favourite, the Adams.

This is a wonderful time of the year for the stream fisherman, and subject to temperature and rainfall it can continue for the greater part of the season. Lake fly-fishers also get in on the act as temperatures rise and have superb fishing around December when the mudeyes move in vast numbers to the shore to hatch out and become the beautiful dragonflies and damsel flies we see flying everywhere before Christmas.

Come summer the grasshoppers multiply like mad and on windy days these get blown onto lakes and into rivers and trout absolutely love these big juicy meals. Fly-fishermen love these insects because they often cause the trout to lose caution and absolutely go for it. At these times fly-fishers use bigger dry flies that look like grasshoppers and slap them down to attract the voracious trout's attention. These are exciting times, a real contrast to some of the subtle presentations that trout demand when smaller, more delicate insects like mayflies and caddis flies are on the menu.

The number of flies that have been invented for different situations is quite mind-boggling. There are tens of thousands. For practical purposes or to create a heated discussion around the camp fire just try suggesting that it is possible to fish the world with only a handful of patterns!

The trick is to identify the insects available to the trout in the area you are fishing. Check in with the local fly shop but remember that a few nymphs and dry flies will normally do the trick. Add a few flies for getting down deep and fishing as attractors, such as Woolly Buggers—especially olive green and black ones—and you are well on the way to fooling most trout that come your way. I have numerous fly boxes with all manner of attractive and exotic flies that have never caught a trout, just me in the fly shop!

Chapter 7

CATCH AND RELEASE

Fly-fishing as a recognised sport has grown tremendously in recent years. Along with this growth we have seen a profound change in anglers' ethics and nowhere more so than in the vital area of conservation.

Only a generation ago we would often see pictures of fishermen with huge smiles standing beside enormous catches. Those were the days when fish were prolific and the attitude seemed to be that success was measured by the numbers of fish killed. Fortunately this view is fast fading and the successful fisherman today limits his catch to what he can legitimately use, with due regard to the current fishing regulations.

The concept of catch and release had its origins in the United States of America and was born of the need to cope with a rapidly increasing number of recreational anglers who were putting tremendous pressure on fish numbers.

A gradual process of education has meant that most fishermen release the bulk of the fish they catch with a view to conserving fisheries for future generations. In the trout fishing scene in America there are anglers who have been fishing for many years and who have never killed a trout and have released every fish caught.

With the growing awareness of the fragility of our environment and more specifically the sensitivity of our rivers and lakes to pollution and land degradation, we are now seeing a whole generation of fishermen that is more respectful of the fish we pursue and much more aware of the problems that intensive farming and industry can have on stream quality and the availability of quality fish. Healthy environment equals healthy streams equals healthy fish—a simple equation that in many parts of the world is increasingly hard to live up to.

As one becomes engrossed in the pursuit of any fish species you cannot help but take an active interest in the life cycle and welfare of the fish itself. As we learn more of a fish's habits we are able to catch them more readily. In the days when catching fish was vital to feeding one's family and thus surviving, knowledge of fish and their habits was essential. Today we find people fishing for reasons other than survival.

Recreational fishing has boomed in the past few decades with fishing now rated as the largest participant sport in Australia. Certainly a lot of fish caught find themselves on the dinner table but a growing number of Australians are limiting their catches and carefully releasing both fresh and saltwater species. Kissing them and putting them back has been popularised by Rex Hunt on his television program and there are very few young people who have not seen Rex kiss and release his fish.

Now I personally draw the line at kissing the trout I catch—I've never been into the piscatorial pout—but putting them back is a great source of pleasure. I occasionally keep a fish if a family member or a friend wants one. Smoked trout is a particular favourite of mine and one or two trout are always sufficient for my purposes. What I find really offensive are the meat fishermen who have no regard for bag limits and who boast about how many fish they caught and how they filled the freezer. These are the same people who end up throwing out most of these fish when they don't use them within their normal freezer life. What a sad and tragic waste.

In the Southern Highlands we have dams like Fitzroy Falls and Pejar up above Goulburn that are stocked with hatchery fish bred by the New South Wales government on a regular basis to make fish available to licensed anglers who want to go out and catch a feed. These fish are usually plentiful and relatively easy to catch. There are bag limits and these should be observed. What sensible person could argue with that?

Our secret creeks are a different matter altogether. These waters are much more fragile and very reliant on seasonal rains or springs to keep them running sufficiently to sustain healthy populations of trout. Local acclimatisation societies stock these streams in an attempt to keep a reasonable number of fish available for recreational anglers. Some of these streams support large numbers of small fish while others have fewer but much larger fish. These few large fish are the ones that provide the ultimate sport and test us to the limit. These are the fish that should always be handled with care and returned as quickly as possible.

All these streams have a certain amount of natural recruitment which means that given the chance these fish are replenishing their own numbers naturally. Remove these large breeding fish and you greatly reduce the chances for wild fish to spawn and in some streams a fisherman who keeps everything he catches will decimate the trout population for years to come. By all means keep a couple of pan sized fish, but take a photograph of the big ones quickly and release them. As famous American fly-fisherman Lee Wulff once famously said 'A trophy fish is far too valuable to catch only once'. The message is: put them back and let them do what nature intended.

Chapter 8

WOLLONDILLY WONDER

Every year many millions of trout and salmon run up rivers to deposit their eggs and so ensure the continuation of salmonid species worldwide. This incredible migration is known as the spawning run. It is a fascinating part of the life cycle of the trout and quite a story in itself. In Australia these migrations are found in large lakes with streams that run into them, like the Eucumbene River that runs into Lake Eucumbene and the delightful Thredbo River that runs into Lake Jindabyne.

With a view to protecting spawning fish there are closed seasons where no fishing is allowed so that the trout can get on with the business of reproducing without being disturbed by fishermen. Generally the closed season in New South Wales for stream fishing is between the June long weekend and the Labour Day long weekend in October. These regulations apply to all declared trout streams and fishing for trout out of season attracts large fines. Lakes on the other hand may be fished year round.

There are some rivers in New South Wales that are not declared trout waters that have a run of trout in winter if the conditions are just right and one of these is the wonderful Wollondilly. The reason these fish are not protected is that the Wollondilly is not a year round trout fishery because the water becomes too warm in summer for trout to survive. The trout live for most of the year in Lake Burragorang, which was created many years ago when Warragamba Dam was built to supply Sydney with water. This lake is ideal for trout, being deep and cold, and has an enormous population of very fit rainbow trout. Lake Burragorang is entirely off limits to fishermen, bushwalkers and the general public because of Sydney Water's desire to keep the area pristine and unpolluted for the supply of water to the Sydney region. This is unfortunate when you consider the access allowed by other water supply authorities worldwide to their water supplies and especially when you consider the incredible natural beauty of Lake Burragorang. Anyway, the authorities see this population of trout as a resource that can be harvested during winter, as they are not concerned with their continued survival in this particular river or in the lake itself.

When autumn arrives the trout's urge to reproduce is aroused. The females become laden with eggs and they tend to school near the entrance of the rivers that flow into the lake. The fish are waiting for nature's message to move upstream and deposit their eggs. This message comes in the form of substantial rainfall high in the catchment areas. The fish need to know that there is a sufficient supply of cold water running down the river to keep their eggs cold and well aerated and they don't run up river unless these rains fall at just the right time. This can cause real problems here in Australia, as winter rainfall in many areas where trout have been introduced is rather unreliable. In the trouts' traditional habitats of North America and Europe the winter rainfall and snow is much more predictable and the seasonal runs of both trout and salmon can often be predicted to within a few days. These fish come in from the ocean to spawn and our rainbow trout are descended from the sea run trout or steelhead as they are known on the American northwest seaboard.

When the flow and temperature of the water is right the trout travel upstream to find suitable gravel beds so that the female can dig a shallow depression in the gravel with her tail. This is called a redd and the eggs are deposited here as the male swims frantically beside her and fertilises the eggs by spraying them with his milt at exactly the time the female deposits them. Immediately this is done, the female uses her tail to cover up the fertilised eggs with the gravel and the tiny eggs are left to mature over a period of several weeks depending on the water temperature.

Of the enormous number of eggs that are deposited only a tiny fraction survive to adulthood but the cycle of life continues with these fish becoming sexually mature at about two years of age. Rainbow trout live for about five years and brown trout often survive for around ten years. Fortunately both these species can reproduce more than once and do not die in enormous numbers like several of the salmon species of North America after their once-only spawn run.

Following some recent rains, local professional guide Mark Tickner and I did a quick research trip and had the good fortune to see some trout on the move and caught a nice specimen well upstream from Burragorang. This fish was sitting deep in a run behind a rock, as many of them do, and grabbed a small olive green nymph as it passed close by. It gave a superb fight and had already spawned so we kept it and had it smoked by Carter's Butchery in Mittagong. Its stomach was full of large green mudeyes, the larval stage of the dragonfly. This proved our hunch was right to use an olive green fly-fished across and downstream with a floating line and suspended on about two metres of leader under a small strike indicator. This rig let the fly wash naturally around the rocks to successfully tempt the trout.

There are a couple of schools of thought about fishing for spawning run fish. The first says you should never fish for them. The second says you should respect the closed season streams but you are justified in fishing for fish that are otherwise unavailable to recreational fishers in undeclared waters where the fish only come up to spawn if the conditions are just right. I lean toward the latter approach, mainly because the fish in the Wollondilly represent such a small proportion of the total fish population in Lake Burragorang. They so rarely come up the Wollondilly that the population in the lake does not depend on this occasional run for their continued survival. Of course you can also practice catch and release in these streams as we invariably do in the declared trout streams.

I would really like to see a sensible approach to public access to Lake Burragorang so the general public could enjoy this spectacularly scenic area so close to Sydney. This would allow responsible fishers to utilise this splendid resource more effectively.

Chapter 9

TIGHT LOOPS

One of the ultimate goals of any fly-fisher should be to become a really competent caster. The surest way to know if a fly-caster is well along the road to masterful casting is to look at the way their line unfurls throughout the cast. With a correct casting action the fly line forms a loop before it straightens out on both the forward and backward cast. These loops need to be reasonably narrow to lessen the resistance of the line to the wind and allow the caster to extend the length of the fly line and put the fly where the fish can see it.

Loop control is arguably the most critical element in turning an average caster into a seriously good presenter of flies. An understanding of how to form tight loops and wide loops and when to combine them opens up a whole new world to the average angler and gives them fish catching opportunities and levels of finesse that will transform their casting and fishing experience.

The expert caster uses an educated wrist and makes casting look both easy and effortless. The loops in the fly line stay high and straight and the only time they open up in size is when the caster lets them. By keeping the rod tip high when you stop the rod in both directions, the line cannot help but stay up in the air and in a narrow loop. The minute you let the rod tip follow too great an arc in either part of the cast, the line will almost certainly hit the ground behind you or slap the water in front. On a typical rocky riverbank this usually results in a lost or broken fly on the rocks behind, or a frightened fish in front.

I remember in my early days of fly-fishing an incident on the glorious Tumut River in New South Wales. I cast a dry fly to a trout five times, got a lovely drag free drift, and remarkably it took the fly every time. I struck five times and the fly never even pricked the trout. In frustration I finally checked the fly and found that the barb and half the bend of the hook were missing. The trout must have been thoroughly mystified at these strange turbo-charged insects flying from inside his closed mouth! From that day on I learnt to keep my back casts high and above those damaging rocks.

One of the best ways to improve your casting is to remember that the fly line always follows the tip of the rod. If you angle the rod sideways as you make your cast, the line follows the tip of the rod and goes quite low backwards and forwards. This is handy for casting under trees or where you think the trout might see the line high in the air, but you have to be even more careful that the line doesn't touch the ground because of the lower casting stroke.

There are times where a wider loop is very useful, particularly when presenting the fly on the final cast. A wide loop means a more gentle presentation. The more delicately you land the fly the more natural it appears to the fish. You can exaggerate the width of the loop by finishing the cast with your rod tip nearly on the water. Assuming it is not windy, the loop unfurls slowly onto the water surface in a series of wiggles rather than in a straight line, with the leader doing the same thing. This is an excellent presentation cast for fishing floating lines and dry flies, particularly upstream. The wiggles in the line are like a shock absorber and prevent the line straightening too quickly in the running water and dragging the fly unnaturally in the process.

It is amazing what a difference this approach alone can make to the catch rate of an angler. Two of my fly-fishing friends, Paul Greethead and Roy Hauptberger, are prime examples of just how important a drag free drift can be. Paul was relatively new to fly-fishing and Roy had only been at it a couple of years longer than Paul. When they first started going fishing together Paul could get his casts with a dry fly onto the stream, but was catching very few fish. Roy on the other hand was braining them with virtually every other cast. Paul was getting a bit exasperated and Roy took his rod and made a quick cast and immediately caught a trout. He released that trout and caught another on the next cast in the next pool. Paul was shaking his head until Roy explained the need to ensure a drag free drift. He then demonstrated the type of cast that allows the line to settle gently on the water with that shock absorber effect in place. Once Paul got a 'wiggle cast' off pat, he started to increase his share of trout fooled into taking his fly, which was now drifting in a natural manner.

In windy conditions in places like our glorious alpine country, casting becomes more difficult particularly where the wind is in your face. Here you have to cast your line high to the rear and then drive a tight loop forward under the wind with sufficient force to get the line to straighten, as well as the virtually weightless leader with the fly attached. An open loop in this situation makes it impossible to cheat the wind and get the leader to extend beyond the end of the fly line. Considerable finesse is needed in a situation like this because you have to push the fly line into the wind but at the same time you need to land the fly gently. If you slap the fly down you will invariably spook the fish. About the only time you want to slap the fly in a sort of crash landing is when fishing grasshopper imitations in summer when the hoppers abound, and this is a bit of a technique in itself.

When the wind is blowing strongly from behind it is preferable to do a fairly low back cast and a big wide open loop on the forward cast by finishing the rod high then dropping the tip. The wind will then straighten out your cast for you and minimise the chance of you hitting yourself with the fly on the way forward.

The loop that all fly-fishers fear is the tailing loop, where the loop collapses somewhere during the forward or backward cast—or both. This is usually caused by the rod tip following the wrong path or the caster trying to overpower the cast at the last second. It is also caused by novice casters who flick the tip of their rods, particularly in the forward cast. The casting motion should bring the power on quickly and smoothly in both the forward and back casts. If the cast is more of a snap or flick than a smooth acceleration then a tailing loop will occur. This usually means the fly will catch the fly line at some point in the cast and a tangle is inevitable. You can minimise the problem, or even get away with it sometimes, if you tilt the rod well away from vertical. However the tailing loop is a disaster waiting to happen, especially if you are casting to the fish of the day and you get tangled!

The best way to cure a tailing loop is to think about the basics of the cast and make sure you cast smoothly and stop the rod between the forward and backward casts. If you ensure the rod loads powerfully at the beginning of each cast and you keep the rod tip travelling in a straight line, tight loops will result, and tailing loops will be a thing of the past.

Chapter 10

EXPECTATIONS

One of my favourite fly-fishing companions is my cousin Bruce Sidebottom. I've often heard it said that you can choose your friends but you can't choose your relatives. Fortunately with Bruce I've been lucky on both counts. We have shared many great adventures together and he has recently retired from his veterinary practice in Ballarat, Victoria. This historic gold mining town in Victoria is where he, with his wife Sue, raised two boys and pursued his passionate interest of diagnosing and treating horses with lameness problems. I know he will be greatly missed professionally, but from a selfish point of view I can't wait, as his frantically busy life will take a major turn around and he will have more time for himself, his family and hopefully his fanatical fly-fishing cousin. Perhaps this is the point of retirement—a time to ponder past achievements then plan for the future and have a little more selfish time for oneself.

I remember reading many years ago, and telling Bruce recently, about a study done in America about longevity in middle class men and what effect retirement age had on life expectancy. The study looked at officers in the armed forces and professionals in the civilian community. The sample was taken from a very large insurance company, so the numbers were considerable and the conclusions they drew on retirement age alone went something like this. The men that retired at sixty five tended to fall off the perch at about sixty seven years. Those that retired at sixty lived on average until seventy three. Those that retired at fifty five were very likely to make their early eighties. A more recent study backed up these figures and suggested that retiring at fifty would see the mid eighties achieved. I just wish they had factored in fly-fishing and early retirement—obviously we should be retiring as early as possible and fly-fishing into our nineties!

I hope Bruce is going to thoroughly prove this theory here in Australia with me to witness it all the way.

Over the years, our fishing friendship has grown, but the most valuable lesson Bruce has taught me is quite simply to have no expectations. All my life I have dreamed about the next trip and all of the trout or other species of fish we would surely catch. I would get very excited and full of anticipation, not just for myself, but for my fishing companions on these trips. If the day or the week didn't produce many fish, I would sometimes take this personally and feel I had failed in some way. I wouldn't let it spoil my trip, but I would try and learn from the experience or the conditions encountered. I would tell myself that I wasn't disappointed but deep down there had been an expectation of some level of success or achievement, and being honest, I would feel a little let down.

Bruce on the other hand would always come along full of cheer, wearing odd-coloured mismatching socks (the wearing of which, according to him are very lucky piscatorially) and insist on eating a banana for breakfast every morning. Anyone who knows about fishing and especially saltwater fishing will tell you that eating a banana is the kiss of death for any subsequent fishing. Men have been thrown out of otherwise best friend's boats when they've pulled out a banana for a quick snack. Individuals get stuck with these superstitions or old wives' tales. They may be true, or they may not. Bruce firmly believes in odd-coloured socks but has no concern for the smell of banana on his hands. He just likes a banana for breakfast and that's that. If he misses out on his everyday banana he is apparently not the same man. What is worse is his casual flaunting of the banana consumption and then proceeding to catch at least as many as anyone else. For a man who says 'have no expectations', Bruce clearly expects to get lucky with the socks, and to catch any species of fish, whether he has consumed his breakfast banana or not!

I guess the real lesson in all of this is to lighten up and have some fun. Smell the roses…all that sort of thing. Trying too hard, or hoping too much, can spoil your day. Gripping the fly rod so hard that you are almost denting the cork, will only lead to casting with too much intensity. Poor presentations and tennis elbow are almost certainties. Gritting and grinding your teeth will only make your dentist wealthier!

Fly-fishing is generally a game of subtlety and finesse, at least physically. From an emotional point of view it should be the total experience which counts and not the number of fish caught, or their size and weight. Expectations, or at least unrealistic expectations, can definitely trap you into a scoring scenario. The success of a trip is suddenly measured by the number of fish caught, rather than the quality of the experience. We have all certainly been guilty of this approach at some time in our fishing lives. Those niggling post-trip doubts are often created because we expect to perform well, and wished to see our friends fare well, and doing well can be bound up somehow in numbers.

Taking Bruce's approach, you have NO expectations, and therefore cannot be disappointed. Wonderful moments which come your way are a bonus, and any day spent fishing is a blessing. It seems simple but it works. Looking back now, and seeing that by being a little more relaxed, and less on the edge, the days definitely flow better when they start out with this healthy attitude. Famous sportspeople commonly state that they perform best when they 'find the zone'. When they try too hard their performance suffers. When they are too casual, they are not at their best. It is somewhere in between that they really perform, and the same is true in fly-fishing, both physically and emotionally.

In fishing, as in life, I think we can sometimes try too hard, and often this can be detrimental to our results. Maybe it is part of the ageing process, or perhaps a gaining of wisdom. Bruce has a concept, which I am discovering, and certainly the contentment, and pleasure, that angling with NO expectation provides, just gets stronger every year.

I wonder if anyone has any statistics for retiring at forty!

Chapter 11

THE SNOOT BUM NYMPH

There are many satisfying moments in fly-fishing, not the least of which is catching a fish on a fly that you've tied, or maybe even designed yourself. Considering how many thousands of recognised flies are in existence it seems hardly necessary to invent more. However as time goes by and inventive anglers search for even more effective patterns we see some of the older patterns fall away and the new heralded in with all sorts of coverage in the fly-fishing press. This exciting search by innovative fly-tiers worldwide constantly breaks new ground, both in salt and freshwater applications.

Some people become particularly proficient in this area of the sport and a well-tied fly is a pleasure to behold. In fact fly-tying can become so engrossing that many people treat this facet of our sport as an end in-itself. Countless hours are spent at the vice and some superb creations result.

For mere mortals like me, the fly-tying is less of an art form than a practical and satisfying part of the whole picture that is fly-fishing. This story revolves around a creation that no one in his or her right mind would call superb. The best description I could imagine would be…effective.

There we were, three fly-fishermen suitably equipped with all the gear, rods held nonchalantly under our arms and each with his fly box out for comparison, heads bowed in contemplation.

The truth was it had been a hard day on the Campbell's River up near Oberon in the high country west of Sydney. In fact it had been very quiet indeed, with no action on the surface. The weather had been warm and overcast and we felt sure it was going to be a very productive day. As enjoyable as trout fishing can be, there are times when the camaraderie of the occasion can be as memorable as the catch. This day was no exception.

Having fished the dry all morning, searching around the willows and letting little Royal Coachmen and Red Tags search any likely lies and runs, we had all drawn a blank. What with the absence of surface activity we decided a council of war was called for over coffee and sandwiches back at the car. Having got the blood sugar and caffeine levels elevated we worked our way upstream and found ourselves standing beside a particularly attractive pool with gently shelving banks and some difficult reeds flanking the edges. A large lichen covered rock ledge on the far side looked inviting where it disappeared below the waterline and encouraged the most gentle of eddies in the slow-moving and mysteriously deep and dark part of this pool.

My friend John had introduced me to fly-fishing many years ago and I still treated him with that particular respect one owes ones mentors—at least most of the time. My other friend Peter was an enthusiastic beginner and was soaking up any information he could glean from the friendly banter.

Deciding a change of tactics was needed I pulled a particularly shaggy nymph from my box and proceeded to tie it on to the leader. Being something of a perfectionist John at once questioned my choice of fly and said something to the effect that it was the most nondescript fly he'd ever seen with its rough hairy appearance and rude construction.

I decided not to take these comments as criticism. At times like this it's best to smile and bow to greater knowledge, particularly as John regularly ties some of the most beautiful nymphs and mayflies you could imagine.

'What is it' John asked. I said 'A Snoot Bum Nymph'! 'A what?' said John—I laughed and continued to show Pete how to tie my favourite and incredibly simple unlocked blood knot. John's impatience started to show and he said, 'Look if you really are going to use that ridiculous thing you must at least ensure that it sinks! Here, give it to me'.

I passed the fly across attached to the four-pound Maxima leader and John took it by the point and put it between his lips drenching it with saliva. 'Now,' he said 'that's the way to get it to sink, no need for any of those fancy dressings—a good suck will do the trick!'

At this I just doubled up with laughter and Pete who was also in the know had the beginnings of tears in his eyes. The master said, 'What are you blokes laughing about?' I said 'Are you quite sure that's how you get it to sink John?' 'Of course it is' said the slightly bewildered master. 'Look, just like this—hold the point between your thumb and forefinger so you don't hook yourself in the lip and suck it like this'. John gave it another really good suck.

Well, this was too much for Pete and I as we felt our legs getting weak at the knees. John with a certain amount of righteous indignation said, 'OK fellas, what's the big joke?'

I said 'John that's a Snoot Bum Nymph!'

'So!' said John.

I said 'John do you remember Pete's old dog called Snoot—you know the one that moults each year.'

'Sure' said John 'I remember her.'

'Well' I said, 'I got the hair for the dubbing in that nymph from Snoot's bum!'

Imagine the look on John's face as he went several shades paler and started spitting and spluttering. It was a look you'd get after being forced to bite into a lemon. It really was a pleasure to see the master lost for words, his face all contorted and pursed.

To add insult to injury I quickly false cast some line and dropped the now very moist Snoot Bum into the eddy by the rock face. You guessed it—an aggressive little brownie snaffled it and was ultimately the only fish of the day.

Fortunately John is a very good sport and only threatened to break both my legs and my precious four weight Sage. I must admit it looked as though I might be in for a swim as I released the plucky little one pounder with John advancing with another wicked look on his face. Suddenly he burst out laughing and said, 'That's the last time you couple of B's will catch me like that!'

We decided to call it a day soon after that episode and I gave John a couple of Snoot Bums when we reached the car. To his credit he graciously accepted them.

If you want to know how to dress this fly it's the same as a small brown or black nymph but with dog hair substituted as the dubbing.

Dear old Snoot has long gone on her way, but as long as I live I will never forget the look of horror on John's face. To this day he doesn't know the hair actually came from the back of her rear leg and not actually from her bum. Poetic license I think that's called. Anyway, we've managed to resist telling him ever since, so if you ever come across a bloke on the Campbells, suspiciously eyeing the nymph he's attaching, ask him discreetly 'Is that a Snoot Bum Nymph?', then start running!

Chapter 12

THE SCIENCE OF FLY-TYING

Fly-tying is a fascinating part of the fly-fisher's repertoire. It can be practised for purely economic reasons or it can be a pastime in itself. Somewhere in between these two extremes, the art of tying your own flies can be a source of great satisfaction and endless experimentation. To fool a fish with a fly of your own creation seems to add a little extra zing to what is already a very exciting experience. Fly-tiers the world over know the degree of satisfaction that comes from this little extra involvement.

Commercially tied flies come in a bewildering number and variety, and are usually more than adequate for the purpose of catching fish. Many fly-tiers satisfy themselves by tying reasonable copies of the most popular and effective flies available commercially. Real enthusiasts set about improving on the classic patterns while other intrepid souls get their greatest buzz by inventing original flies for their own particular purposes. A few of these flies make their inventors famous and they become part of fly-fishing history.

Fly-tying can be a reasonably simple task where functional flies are concerned. At the other end of the spectrum we see the hand tied marvels that are genuine works of art such as the classic and colourful Atlantic salmon flies which can sell to collectors for thousands of dollars. The minute imitations of mayflies and other terrestrial insects are also a testament to the skill of their creators. Each fly has its own purpose and some are simple and impressionistic while others are remarkably lifelike and tied with all manner of materials, both natural and synthetic, to get the effect the fly-tier is seeking.

Starting in fly-tying is a relatively inexpensive exercise where the basic tools and materials are purchased from a specialist fishing shop. Basic fly-tying kits are available for both fresh and saltwater flies and are an affordable way to get all the basics to begin with. There are many good books available on the subject to help the novice and expert alike. Two of my favourite Australian publications are Peter Leuver's *Fur and Feather* and *Australia's Best Trout Flies* by Malcolm Crosse and Rob Sloane. Both books are superbly presented and particularly relevant because of their Australian content. These books illustrate the flies and outline the materials, hooks and provide the tying instructions required to construct flies that really catch trout. They also provide fascinating bits of information about the history of the flies and how they came to be.

The sky is the limit when one graduates from beginner to enthusiast. Fabulous materials are available from various corners of the world including the capes from specially bred roosters from America for tying exquisite hackled dry flies. The tiny feather from the rooster is tied to the front of the hook and wound around behind the eye of the hook to create the circle of fibres that keep the fly erect on the surface of the water where the trout hopefully mistakes it for a natural insect. There are some seriously weird ingredients that have been used to make flies and some of the best came from endangered animals which are now protected, and rightly so. Seals' fur substitutes are now available, as are plastic jungle cock feathers. All manner of synthetic materials are now used to create flies that are almost as good as the real thing.

As one would expect, there are various schools of thought on natural materials versus synthetics, with many people believing only the natural materials make the ultimate flies for fooling our speckled friends. This is not an argument I'm ready to buy into, but I have to admit the yellow rubber legs on a Tassie Tarantula look pretty good and the trout seem to think so too! Come to think of it, the eyes on the Aussie Patriot with its gold tinsel ribbing wrapped over the dyed olive green rabbit's fur body are certainly very striking (see *Australia's Best Trout Flies* by Malcolm Crosse and Rob Sloane).

Of course there are times when the trout can be unbelievably fussy and it becomes imperative to match the hatch. Sometimes the size of the fly can make all the difference. At other times it is the colour or shape that matters. When insects are hatching out and the trout are feeding at the surface there is little time to spare. A competent angler observes the insect activity and presents a fly that generally looks the part—and keeps his fingers crossed. If his offering is consistently refused and the trout is not scared and remains feeding, then a smaller version of the same fly or perhaps something similar will prove to be his undoing. Getting a fish to accept your fly can be easy one day and unbelievably frustrating the next.

I guess a word of warning is in order: this fly-tying thing can get a little out of control. You can find yourself trying to grapple with all the scientific names of insects and laying awake at night agonising over the perfect fly to fool that huge and over-educated brown trout in your favourite secret creek. You may even find yourself haunting haberdashery shops, eyeballing small buttons, beads and natural coloured cottons. Worse still, you start hoarding yellow baling twine because there is simply nothing better for grasshopper legs!

If you have read this far you are probably past the point of no return and no amount of counselling will help. Just remember to be careful with your neighbour's black Labrador. Don't be too greedy and make the haircut too obvious. It's very hard to convince rational people that the hairs on their precious dogs back leg can be spun around a tiny hook and create the most perfect black nymph bodies imaginable.

Chapter 13

DAWN PATROL

There seems to be an unwritten rule in fly-fishing that says the serious angler should be at the water at first light. This is particularly true of lake fishing but it flies in the face of the historically accurate rule of thumb that says the best time to fish for trout is when it is most comfortable for the angler. Now I know this all sounds a bit confusing but that is what fishermen are taught from an early age and there is a certain masochistic charm in waking to a jangling alarm in the pitch black of early morning, then travelling miles to a favoured fishing spot in the freezing cold and arriving as the light comes up and the world around you awakens. Whether or not it is right, we get out of bed early with hope in our hearts, and sometimes we are rewarded—very richly rewarded.

The whole 'early bird catches the worm' theory with trout fishing revolves at least in part around the idea that the trout are more inclined to feed in the very early morning at first light because this minimises the risk of predators spotting them in the shallows. The same theory says the other good time from a trout's point of view is last light in the evening for the same reasons. This is a very simplistic approach and works best at the times of year when the early morning and late evening are the most comfortable for the trout and that is more a function of water temperature not predation. That time of the year is high summer.

This is where the rule of thumb comes in for angler comfort being the same as trout comfort. Trout like cool conditions and need cool well-oxygenated water to survive. When the water gets too warm the oxygen level drops and the trout retreat to the cooler depths or die. Fishermen are also affected by the weather and the most pleasant time to fish during summer is in the cool of early morning, or late evening as the temperature drops. Equally the most comfortable time in winter is during the middle of the day when things have warmed up a little.

Aquatic and land born insects are temperature dependant and are often most active when the temperature is most comfortable for them. Active insects usually mean active trout, either on the surface if the insects are hatching, or sub-surface for the rest of the time. Knowledgeable anglers know about these things—or at least they think they do. They plan their fishing trips around a particular time of year and what seems the most productive time of the day. If all goes to plan it usually goes very well indeed.

However like all plans, they don't always come off. This is both the charm and frustration of fly-fishing. What should be predictable is sometimes anything but predictable. Any number of variables can pop up and wreck the best of plans. A sudden change of wind direction or a drop in barometric pressure can turn the hatches and fish right off. An easterly on the Monaro is usually the end of dry fly-fishing for the wily brown trout in this south eastern corner of New South Wales. A southerly buster on the coast invariably shuts down the saltwater fishing at any time or tide.

Let's face it, if everything ran like clockwork then it would be fine for a while but would ultimately become boring. The challenge is in reading the conditions and putting into effect a set of strategies that are well thought out and that ultimately prove to be the trout's undoing. With all the knowledge and expertise in the world there are still days when everything looks perfect yet the fishing is hopeless. We all have these days and just being there is usually compensation in itself.

Just recently I was fishing the last week of the season on the Thredbo with a group of our FFISH members. No—that's not a spelling stutter—FFISH stands for Fly-fishers in The Southern Highlands and causes lots of laughs when we refer to our wives and girlfriends as FFISHWIVES—well at least we think it's funny. I decided to try my luck for an hour or so in Hatchery Bay on Lake Jindabyne, where the day before one of our guys caught a one kilogram brook trout and another a small Atlantic salmon. The lake was low, the weed beds were visible and the water looked superb. I was having a very happy time dead-drifting a couple of small nymphs on a long leader attached to a floating line when it suddenly occurred to me that I was fishing in a strong easterly. I wasn't catching any fish but just enjoying being there when it dawned on me why it was so quiet: the dreaded easterly. The day before the boys had a westerly in the same bay and the fish were active.

Most fly-fishers would agree that the early morning is a magic time of day. The dawn patrol is a perfect time to enjoy all the other parts of fishing that fall into the category of just being there. This is the time on a cold winter morning where the sun rises to reveal a blue-sky day but the fishermen find themselves engulfed in a dense white cloud on the lake foreshore that doesn't burn off until at least 9.30 am. This is surreal fishing at its best. You can't see more than six or seven metres in any direction and the searching fly lands out of sight. That it does this at all is something of a miracle as you can barely feel your fingers for the cold. Water birds drift casually out of the grey wall of mist and into view at very close range and disappear just as quickly when they realise there is a stranger on the scene. The water is invariably glassy calm and as the mist lifts, the slightest disturbance is easily spotted in the mirror-like surface. The sheer beauty takes your mind away from the fishing until a subtle rise nearby grabs your attention. The hunt is on and the surrounding scenery takes a temporary back seat to the action close at hand.

So many non-anglers assume the reason for fly-fishing is to catch fish to eat, and that's all. The real reasons are so much more. Just being there is tremendously important. Catching a wily fish is almost a bonus. I feel sure that serious fly-fishers get to a stage where some kind of reverse psychology kicks in and they go fishing because the fish has actually caught them! In a physical sense we hook the trout but really we can't wait to find an excuse to go fishing because it is we that are truly hooked.

I've heard people say that fishing is an escape from reality. Those anglers who love the dawn patrol know that in this crazy world full of power hungry politicians, terrorists, sprawling polluted cities and impossibly hectic schedules, the pure and simple pleasures of fly-fishing and the places where fish live, are actually an escape to reality.

Chapter 14

STRIKE!

Fly-fishing is a magical mixture of casting, presentation of the fly and ultimately, deception. We anglers spend years, often a lifetime, honing our skills and learning to present flies naturally in an effort to fool our much-loved quarry. We make a satisfying cast that leaves the fish unaware of our presence, while putting the fly in a position to float down the stream naturally without dragging and giving the game away. The trout spots the fly and in a moment decides to eat it. Everything seems to go into slow motion as the fish glides up to the surface, its mouth opening before it takes the fly. The critical moment is upon us—how long do we wait until we strike? How long before the fish realises it has been fooled and spits out the fly? All the preparation and practice, and it comes down to this: when do I strike?

This must be one of the most asked questions in the world of fly-fishing, and the answer is anything but simple. In dry fly fishing where the take is visual, because you can see the fly floating, the answer varies from immediately to three or four seconds. In the high drama of the moment a wait this long seems like an eternity. Some anglers swear by silently saying 'God save the Queen' before they strike. Others believe that any delay at all will see the fly rejected and the fish spooked. The fact is that all these answers are right. In sub-surface nymph fishing you strike when you feel the fish take the submerged fly or you see the indicator go under. It is important that you strike immediately. There is never a reason to delay.

There are some rules of thumb that apply to dry fly fishing and they go something like this. Big fish tend to take more slowly than small fish. Big fish tend to dominate their stretch of stream and can afford to be both more selective and relaxed. Smaller fish tend to be more opportunistic and need to grab whatever they can. Big fish by virtue of their size tend to take longer to turn down once they have taken the fly. Little fish seem to turn over a fly faster and need to be hooked more quickly.

OK—I did say these are rules of thumb. There are times when big fish take flies quickly and this tends to relate to what the natural insects are doing. In grasshopper season both the smaller fish and the big ones seem to engulf the fly at the earliest opportunity. When the mayflies are on, it is often a more leisurely affair as mayflies spend some time at the surface of the water either hatching out or laying their eggs. When dragonflies are about the trout can be infuriating in that they launch themselves out of the water chasing these electric blue insects as they hover above the water. Going on my observations, they get the dragonflies and damsels a fair percentage of the time.

Each situation demands a different timing. As if fly-fishing isn't difficult enough I hear you say! Of course it was an Australian Prime Minister Malcolm Fraser who said 'life wasn't meant to be easy' and he may as well have been talking about his favourite recreation away from Parliament—fly-fishing for trout.

It takes time and experience to learn the various strikes and even then there is a bit of luck involved. The beginner invariably has trouble connecting with fish in the early days, but with time and experience hook-up rates improve. Golfers often get the 'yips' with their putting, and fly-fishers can experience the same problems by getting overexcited and striking before the fish has actually taken the fly. This can be very funny for an observer but the angler is often mortified. Such is the anticipation and tension of the moment in dry fly fishing.

One of the hardest things for a fly-fisher to do is to research this issue. Nerves of steel and the ability to put years of habit behind you are required. You must present the fly to the fish and observe it take the fly—but you must not strike—not at all. This is one of the hardest things in the fly-fishing world to do. It simply goes against all your instincts and years of fishing. Let the fish take the fly and count in seconds how long it takes to reject your little deception. In really clear water this can actually be a lot of fun as you can see the look on the fishes face as it realises its mistake and for all the world looks disgusted and ejects the fly in a disdainful millisecond! I can't say for sure that fish have facial expressions, and perhaps it is my imagination when I say they look disgusted as they spit out the fly. The fact is they don't take very long to realise that what they've taken is a deception, so out it comes.

Little fish seem to eject the fly very quickly while many bigger fish seem to take as much as five or six seconds. Of course it varies between fish, and you can only take so much of this unselfish research before you cannot resist getting connected!

Fly-fishing is a never-ending learning curve and the perfectly timed strike can seem as elusive as some Holy Grail. Fortunately for us mere mortals, an imperfectly timed strike will often get the result we want—a few minutes connected to a vibrantly coloured and energetic fish, and the chance to be a part of nature in a very special way.

Chapter 15

A NEW MILLENNIUM

When the fabulous fireworks exploded over Sydney for the celebration of New Year 2001, we also celebrated entry to a new millennium. A new thousand years and all this holds for our personal futures, and that of mankind. Mind expanding stuff to be sure, and a little daunting if you stop long enough to think about it.

Of course fly-fishers are noted for stopping and thinking. Izaak Walton, in his remarkable work *The Compleat Angler*, first published in 1653, later described his book as 'the contemplative mans recreation'. This literary classic must be one of the most read and reprinted works on fishing the world has ever seen. Much of what Walton had to say in his five revised and expanded editions about the allure of angling are equally relevant today. As we contemplate the new millennium from a fishing perspective we have a lot to look forward to and a great deal to learn from the last thousand years.

It is hard to imagine that we could see much improvement in the technology of the late twentieth century in terms of the outstanding equipment with which we fish, but we doubtless will. On the other hand, it is not difficult to look back and realise we have our work cut out for us in the future in terms of population pressures and the environmental degradation fisheries have suffered worldwide.

In fishing, as in life, everything seems to go in cycles. For trout fishers there are boom and bust seasons. Some years there seem to be fish aplenty; others there are very few. All of this can be attributed to something as all encompassing as the recent drought periods associated with the infamous El Nino weather patterns or something as simple as individual greed and keep-and-kill fishing in a particularly sensitive secret creek.

Very late in the last millennium Rex Hunt appeared on Australian television screens, inspiring a generation of young children to go fishing and to kiss the fish and put them back. This was something of a shock to the parents and grandparents of these young fishers who themselves had been taught to keep whatever they caught, or at the very least, keep the big ones and throw back the small ones. That was all very well in their day, but inappropriate as we cast our way into the twenty-first century. Kissing them and putting them back is a simple way of saying we must respect and appreciate the fish we catch and put back the large fish because they got that way by being the strongest individuals and they are often the big breeding females of the species. This is just one example of what we need to be doing to enhance and protect our fishing for future generations.

From an environmental perspective it is very fortunate that trout inhabit some of the most beautiful places on Earth. Trout species need clear cold well-oxygenated water to allow them to breed and prosper. Anglers are forming groups to lobby governments both here in Australia and around the world to protect these regions from over exploitation and environmental degradation. Something as simple as a passion for trout fishing is leading to the protection of vast areas of trout habitat worldwide and this movement will continue to grow.

With the recent explosion of interest in fly-fishing we have seen some interesting changes in the demographics of angling, that is in the type of people who enjoy fly-fishing. Gone are the elitist notions of fly-fishing. Today we are as likely to see a young bricklayer discussing the best fly with a retired surgeon along a stream or lake foreshore. Tweed jackets and ties have been largely replaced with purpose-designed, lightweight, colour co-ordinated fishing clothing. Polaroid glasses and broad-brimmed hats are now vital parts of the angler's kit whether he fishes high alpine regions or tropical sand flats. With the growth of saltwater fly-fishing as a viable alternative to traditional methods of fishing for marine species we see a change in focus from the image of the fly-fisher chasing trout to a more encompassing view of fly-fishing.

In this new millennium we are seeing a lot more of the saltwater scene as fly-fishing methods are perfected for many of our saltwater game fish. We have for many years had trout fishing competitions on a local and international basis. Many trout fishing traditionalists are horrified at the very thought of competition entering into our sport. This is certainly an issue for the future, and one which stirs up a veritable hornets' nest around the campfire or in the fishing press. I feel certain that Izaak Walton would turn in his grave at the thought of competing with one another to catch the most or largest fish in a given period of time. At least nowadays these competitions are catch and release and the keep and kill competitions are virtually a thing of the past.

The World Fly-fishing Championships held at Jindabyne in 1999 were an enormous success in terms of shared information between competitors, organisers and various state bodies charged with the wellbeing of fish and fisheries in this unique part of Australia. In this sense competitions will be a useful part of our future.

While we look forward to the future of our sport and the growth of the saltwater scene it is worthwhile remembering why our forefathers took up the sport and what it meant to them. Nowhere is this more perfectly encapsulated for me than in 'An Angling Song' from *The Gentleman's Recreation* by Nicholas Cox, 1677.

> 'Come lay by your cares, and hang up all sorrow
> Lets Angle today, and ne're think of tomorrow;
> And by the Brook-side as we angle along,
> Wee'l cheer up our selves with our sport and a song.
>
> Sometimes on the Grass our selves we will lay,
> And see how the watery Citizens play,
> Sometimes with a fly stand under a tree,
> And chuse out what Fish our captives will be.
>
> Thus void of all care we're more happy than they
> That sit upon Thrones and Kingdoms do sway;
> For Sceptres and crowns disquiet still bring,
> But the man that's content is more blest than a King.'

Written over three hundred years ago this angling song never fails to inspire and remind me of the real attraction of fly-fishing. As we look forward to the future, it is the past that provides much of our security and solace. For fly-fishers the past is a rich tapestry and the future a blank canvas. Welcome to an exciting new millennium.

Chapter 16

IMITATION VERSUS PRESENTATION

One of the age old questions in fly-fishing is whether imitation or presentation of the fly is the most important factor in successfully fooling and catching a trout. Experienced fly-fishers the world over have persuasively argued the case for both positions and everyone who takes their fly-fishing seriously will eventually be drawn into this controversy.

The imitationist assumes reasonable skill on the angler's part and believes that the trout rises to his flies because of their close likeness to the insects hatching and being eaten by the trout. The presentationist graciously attributes the success of the imitationist to his angling skills and not his superbly tied flies, the argument being that it matters not how perfectly the fly replicates the insect, but how it is presented in a lifelike and natural manner. If you want to stir up a hornets' nest around the campfire this is a beauty. Many anglers will argue black and blue for one side or the other.

All this assumes that there has to be one side or another. I'm prepared to stick my neck out and say the truly successful angler combines the two. In my defence I must defer to a higher authority and say I am greatly indebted to one of the grand old men of fly-fishing in Australia for his views on the subject, the late John Sautelle, who fished extensively with the fly both in his beloved Monaro streams in south eastern New South Wales and in some of the world's most exotic and revered fly-fishing locations.

In a 1988 edition of *Freshwater Fishing Australia* John Sautelle recounted a fabulous story depicting the importance of imitation by Vince Marinaro, author of *In the Ring of the Rise*. The story concerned a trout which, after many failures, Marinaro christened 'the untouchable'. Having cast a hundred or more times to this particular fish and having been ignored on every occasion Marinaro decided to just sit and try to figure out why this fish was so uncooperative and apparently such a gourmet. He found the fish was feeding on only one insect, a common housefly and he traced the source of these flies to a dung heap by an upstream barn!

From intense observation Marinaro discovered that not every natural fly that floated over the trout was accepted and so began a laborious tying of reasonable facsimiles by the streamside. Then began 'the game of nods'. Every time an artificial fly was presented and the fish showed any interest it would nod its head either by looking up at the fly or rising to the fly and following it closely and examining it minutely but not taking it. In the end the flies that received the greatest interest were rated as such, and a fly was tied that combined their various features. Finally the 'untouchable' took this masterpiece of fly-tying and patience, and Marinaro attributed his success to the addition of hackle fibres that imitated the fly rubbing its forefeet together. What a shame the fish came unstuck and Marinaro failed to land it after all that effort!

No one would deny that this extraordinary story illustrates the importance of imitation, but to my mind it also suggests that Vince Marinaro must have been unbelievably skilful in his presentation to have made all those casts and not scared the fish. His abilities as a fly-tyer must have been enormous and his levels of determination and patience beyond belief. Fooling that fish must have been a great thrill but it would seem to me that a combination of factors were at play both in terms of imitation and presentation. It may just have been a case of the fish finally deciding to take the fly for no reason whatsoever. Or perhaps all those cunningly tied flies eventually fooled the trout into thinking that what was being presented so consistently was some new kind of insect hatch and he had better try one … who really knows? It certainly is a good story.

In the Southern Highlands and Snowy Mountains regions of New South Wales we can catch trout by imitating the life cycles of various insects throughout the season and that proves we are in part following the imitationist credo. This is never more so than in the warmer months when we see Christmas beetles or grasshoppers making up the major part of the trouts' diet. Patterns that replicate these insects are virtually a must at these times. These large bite sized morsels need, however, to be presented properly or the fish will see through our little ruse. They should be slapped down sufficiently on the water like a natural falling onto the stream and they are even more effective if we can impart some life into them by moving the rod tip or twitching the fly line—that's the importance of presentation. So that makes us presentationists as well!

When we are impersonating mayflies, we want the fly to land near the trout as delicately as possible—that is how the fish would expect a mayfly to land and to be travelling down the stream—with no drag. Slap the mayfly down and the game will surely be over. Emerging mayflies float downstream while their wings are drying and are at the complete mercy of the trout for these few minutes of their life cycle. Certainly this is how the fish in our secret creeks respond to a natural or unnatural drift and we all need to be mindful of the need to combine imitation and presentation if we are to fool some of these very large and cunning old trout.

The ultimate experience for fly-fishers around the world is fishing for trout we can see. Large browns and rainbows cruise in our creeks and dams when the conditions are favourable, and this is the 'champagne fly-fishing' that John Sautelle wrote about so evocatively. To successfully fool these magnificent creatures takes a very cautious approach, thoughtful imitation and skilful presentation.

I've had so many adventures with my friends over the years where a combination of skills were needed to fool the wary trout. I remember a day with Roy Hauptberger on a tiny tributary of the famous Eucumbene River. It was late in the season and the wind was howling down that alpine valley. It was all we could do to get casts into the tight spots where the trout were lying along the banks of the Eucumbene, and we finally gave up and sneaked up this tiny creek which was sheltered by a high hard rocky ridge. We laughed and said we wondered if such a tiny stream would hold any trout of catchable size but we were tired of being buffeted and thought we'd give it a try. The nameless creek was only a foot or two wide in places and as little as a foot deep. We worked our way up about fifty metres to find a small pool that looked promising. It was surrounded by bushes but a carefully placed cast would give a drag free drift of several metres over the deepest section. It was Roy's turn and he put on a small Adams as we thought this would be the best bet for imitating what might be around so late in the season—a nondescript fly that can be so successful at almost any time of the year. The cast needed to be perfect in such confined surrounds and Roy didn't disappoint. His short three weight drove the floating line in a tight loop and stopped the cast short to allow the fly to land gently in the head of the small pool. Fortunately I had the video recording over his shoulder and we captured the whole event. As the fly drifted down into the pool the current pulled it to the right and fortunately Roy had got enough wiggle into his cast because the second before it was due to drag unnaturally it was clipped from the surface and the fight was on. We were whooping with excitement as the lovely rainbow fought bravely in his small watery domain and Roy finally got him out for us to admire and release. Not a giant, but a good sized fish that we would have been happy with from the river. In this tiny creek we felt like it was a monster and a huge achievement to find it and winkle it out for a few short moments fight and then admiration and release.

Chapter 17

READING THE WATER

With the much anticipated opening of the stream fishing season, we find ourselves full of optimism and eager to set forth. Keen to get our fix of clear running water and fighting fit trout. Gone are the cold, short days of winter and the stream closures that protect the trout while they go about the vital business of spawning and creating another generation. Along the way we need to remember all of the stream-craft we have learnt over the years—the sort of information that is not acquired instantly the first time an angler pulls on their waders. Time, experience and an enquiring mind are essential to come to grips with what is often called 'reading the water'. Like an open book, a stream can be read and analysed and the likelihood of fish being present in certain locations can be predicted with a fair degree of accuracy.

Two of the most important factors that determine a trout's location and indeed survival in a stream are cover and water flow. Cover in the form of deeper water, or some sort of structure like rocks or an overhanging or fallen tree, can make the difference between life and death. Predators are always on the lookout for an easy feed and any trout that is too relaxed or careless is invariably eaten. Water flow is important in terms of oxygenating the water and carrying food items to the waiting trout. In a substantial stream the trout establish a pecking order and station themselves in places where they have reasonable protection and a good food supply. The biggest trout are found in the prime spots and the smaller fish make do as best they can. Survival of the fittest is alive and well in the highly efficient world of the trout.

It is often said that ninety per cent of the trout live in ten per cent of the water. Taken literally this means that unless you know what parts of a stream are represented in that ten per cent then you stand a very poor chance of catching anything at all. Equally interesting is the rule of thumb that says ten per cent of anglers catch ninety per cent of the trout! What do all these figures mean? It means simply that anglers who take the trouble to learn where and why trout occupy certain parts of a stream will always catch, and hopefully release, the lion's share of the available fish.

Learning to read a stream is a vital part of the challenge of unlocking the mysteries of trout fishing. Whether you fish with bait, spinners or fly, the rules are the same. The techniques vary but the fish tend to follow the same rules. In a fast flowing river the trout invariably face upstream as this allows them to pass the water through their mouths and over their gills to most efficiently get the oxygen they need to survive. Food is carried to trout by the stream currents, and this is part of the equation of the trout's efficient use of nature, in the game of calories gained versus calories expended. Trout will always take up a station in an efficient part of the stream where they expend a minimum of energy to harvest the maximum amount of food. Obvious spots will be in the lee of a boulder or behind an old tree stump in the cushioned area of water created by the upstream obstruction. These spots are very energy efficient and usually also provide the cautious trout with the protection they seek by natural instinct.

First or last light are both particularly good periods for trout fishing and this relates in part to the fact that trout have no eyelids. As the day gets progressively brighter the fish will usually go to the deeper parts of a river or position themselves in shady locations. With this sort of knowledge we can accurately predict where the bulk of the fish are during the day. Look for shady spots where the currents channel food near structure and you are probably looking at the magical ten per cent of the stream. The other ninety per cent of the stream, which may be very attractive to us, is often completely barren of fish during broad daylight hours.

As the day nears its end and the sun goes down behind the hills, there is often an evening rise. This is a magic period when many trout seem to cast off their inhibitions with a short but frantic period of feeding before nightfall. This is an intensely exciting time when the smooth broad surfaces of the slow flowing tail ends of pools are often dimpled by trout eagerly feeding on a hatch of caddis or mayfly. This is the time that the skilful angler ties on an imitative dry fly and gently drops it above the ring created on the water surface by one particular rising fish. The anticipation is agonising until the fish either gently sips down your fly—or rejects it. This is very visual fishing and all the more exciting because everything seems to happen in slow motion.

I've often heard it said that to be a successful fisherman you should think like a trout. With a brain the size of a pea no one has ever suggested trout are intellectual giants. What trout lack in brain size they certainly make up for with their incredible sensitivity and perfect adaptation to their environment. To improve our chances of success we must use our bigger brains to imagine the physical needs of the trout and superimpose these over the physical features of the stream to find the most likely locations.

Thinking about those ninety per cent rules, I wouldn't mind betting that the trout have a few rules of their own. In fact I'm sure they win the battle of 'who is really fooling who' against we big brained anglers at least ninety per cent of the time! I for one wouldn't have it any other way.

Chapter 18

A GENTLE HAND

In all forms of fishing it is important to learn fish handling skills once we start to catch a fish or two. Anyone who goes fishing should respect their catch, and obey the rules that apply in their state or territory with respect to licenses and the amount of fish they can keep, including the minimum size and the methods used in their capture.

In fly-fishing we find that many anglers practice catch and release both in fresh and saltwater environs, and never actually kill any of the fish they fool into taking their artificial flies. I read somewhere recently that there is a whole generation of fly-fishers in America that has only ever practised catch and release. Their fish handling skills need to be rather different to the angler that intends killing his catch because their aim is to release the fish with the minimum level of stress. Anglers who keep their fish should kill and clean them immediately, and keep them cool to ensure they get home in good condition so that they can be enjoyed as a tasty and nutritious meal.

The catch and release angler needs to do a number of things to ensure the fish are returned with the very best possible chance of survival. Foremost amongst these is to play the fish quickly and return it to the water as soon as possible. This can be achieved by using reasonably strong tippet material and a net to speed up the capture. Of course this can be a little tricky with fly-fishing for trout where tiny flies are used and fine line is needed to attach the fly and fool the trout. Technology helps here with stronger fine line available nowadays, but still the message is to get the fish in quickly.

The use of a net is also an excellent idea where fish are to be released. Not only does it speed up the capture but also it means that the fish does not even need to be touched while the fly is removed. The best nets today have a special soft mesh that further protects the fish and minimises any damage to their skin and protective mucous membrane—that's the part that makes fish slippery. This membrane is a natural barrier to infection that we would do well not to remove if we want to further enhance the fish's survival rate when practising catch and release. It is also important to wet your hands if you intend to touch a fish so that your otherwise dry hands don't remove any of this membrane. Personally I like to handle fish as part of the whole experience of being in touch with nature so am always careful to wet my hands prior to touching them.

Large fish need special treatment when being lifted out of the water to protect their organs from being stressed. We often see big fish being held up by the jaw and this is fine if they've been killed for the table but not so good if they are to be released. The idea is to provide them with as much support as possible and after a quick photograph they should be returned to the water immediately where their weight and bulk are more perfectly cushioned.

When actually handling fish prior to release it is important to hold them firmly around their tail and rest the bulk of their body on your other hand to provide the support we've already talked about. Alternatively you can swap the tail grip for a jaw grip as long as the fish is not a toothy beast like many of the saltwater fish around our coastline, and you still support it with your other hand. Either of these grips around the tail or the jaw ensure the fish is not dropped onto the ground or into the boat. Accidents will happen but generally fish secured in this way remain unharmed and can be returned to the water quickly and revived very successfully.

Another good trick with trout in particular is to turn them upside down, and this invariably stops them struggling. The reasons for this are unclear but I guess they are simply disorientated, and it does further speed up the process of unhooking a fish prior to righting it and getting a quick photograph.

With trout caught in fast running streams it is always a good idea to gently hold the fish submerged with its head facing upstream during the recovery phase so the highly oxygenated water can flow through its mouth and gills and speed up recovery. Of course it is important to make sure you are not holding the fish in such a way that the gills cannot open and close. You'd be surprised how often this happens with well meaning anglers who think that by holding the fish underwater it can breathe. They hold the fish firmly around the head and this keeps the gills locked shut. If you do this, the fish can't breathe even though you are holding its head underwater. In still water it is often a good idea to move the fish backwards and forwards to simulate the upstream situation and get a flow of water through the gills. Both these processes can take a minute or two and it gives the angler and any onlookers the opportunity to observe these splendid creatures and wonder at their streamlined shape and spectacular colours and markings.

When fish recover you are left in no doubt. One moment you are cradling a subdued creature and suddenly they are gone. A sudden pulse of energy fires a powerful flick of their tail and you part company. It is one of the magic moments in fly-fishing to see a beautiful creature returned so confidently to its own environment.

Handling fish in the way described is not limited to trout fishing. All sports-fish should be treated with the utmost respect and appreciated for what they are—wonders of evolution—and worth all our efforts to study and conserve. In this way we will ensure their survival and pass on viable populations for future generations to enjoy, respect and care about.

Chapter 19

THE FASCINATION
OF BRIDGES

Ask anyone who has driven in a car with a freshwater fisherman what happens when the fisherman spots any sort of moving water. The answer is invariably a sudden change in focus from the road to the water. With any luck the driver will pull over to keep the passengers safe.

To non-anglers this fascination with water seems a mystery, and is particularly puzzling when the object of their angling partner's attention is often nothing more than the tiniest creek that couldn't possibly hold any fish. Still, hope springs eternal and any serious fisher can't resist appraising water. Any potential fish holding lie is scrutinised and speculated upon. This is actually great fun if the other passengers have fishing blood in their veins or some sort of genetic predisposition to becoming addicted to fishing. If they haven't got the bug, then they can only look on with a mixture of disbelief and amazement.

The only thing more attractive to a fisherman than potential water is a creek with a bridge over it. One minute you can be sailing along thinking blissful passenger type thoughts and admiring the view when suddenly the car is braking and then abandoned in the well-worn parking space invariably found on either side of a bridge. The fisherman is out in a flash with a mumbled apology—or no explanation at all—and heads for the centre of the bridge and leans over the railing looking down into the creek. Believe me, this is standard procedure with all the fly-fishers I know—there is something magnetic about bridges.

While fishermen look longingly over bridges and often start their fishing forays at bridge crossings, very few actually fish the bridge. In their eagerness to get upstream or down they often miss the biggest fish in that particular section of the creek. While a bridge is designed for cars and pedestrians to cross it also provides shelter for fish by way of its pylons and shade. These attributes are commonly referred to by fisher folk as structure and fish know a good safe hidey-hole when they see one.

Many fishermen dismiss fishing at points of access like road crossings and bridges, thinking that every man and his dog will have flogged the water and that any sensible fish will be way up or downstream away from the madding crowd—or at least away from those mad fly-fishers!

This makes sense in a convoluted sort of way...except that logic and fly-fishing do not always go hand in hand. Heavily fished spots are often heavily fished within a reasonable walk up or downstream of a bridge. Less pressured water is often well beyond what the average fisherman is prepared to walk, or ironically, right at the bridge. Virtually no one approaches a bridge in the same stealthy manner that they would apply to any other part of a promising stream. They bowl up to the bridge as we've seen already and look upstream or down. They skyline themselves on the bridge and then beat a hasty path up or downstream, whichever takes their fancy. I know I've done this enough times myself. If on the other hand, you park beyond the bridge and give it a wide berth by going downstream you can then approach from below the bridge and with the aid of polarised glasses you might be very surprised by what is finning quietly in the shade under the bridge and completely oblivious to your presence.

Of course having this knowledge and the patience to see the fish is one thing, but catching it can be quite another. These fish are often several seasons old and as wise as a fish can be considering they have brains the size of a pea (which in itself doesn't say much about we fishermen when we get outsmarted by these intellectual giants...but that's another story).

Some small bridges make casting very difficult and to avoid spooking the fish it is often necessary to get the fly under the bridge and into the shade. A tight loop is needed to deliver the fly line under the bridge but sometimes the better option is to float a fly down under the bridge from upstream. This can be a real challenge and the difference between catching the fish and catching the bridge can be a matter of inches.

The sight of a plucky little dry fly floating out of the shadow of the bridge and being enveloped by a serious trout is the stuff of fly-fishing dreams. It is not uncommon for two or three trout to be stationed under a bridge and it is particularly exciting when they all come after your fly. I've had the same experience with bass over the years. I've had as many as five fish appear in squadron formation in order of size or pecking order with the largest in the lead and the smallest at the rear. This can make for a few very visual and exciting moments. You find yourself willing the biggest fish to take the fly. If you placed the fly with a minimum of disturbance and got a good drag free drift, the biggest fish will often follow for quite a distance before making up its mind. It is not uncommon for one of the smaller upstarts to forget the pecking order and race forward and intercept the fly before the dominant fish has made up its mind.

Such is life. At least you fooled one of them! Now you know where the big one lives. Maybe next visit you will make another perfect cast under the bridge and add a little to his education by catching and releasing him. At the very least it will provide the chance for one of those rare victories where big brain overcomes pea-sized brain and gives one the opportunity to tell a suitably embellished 'big one that didn't get away' story.

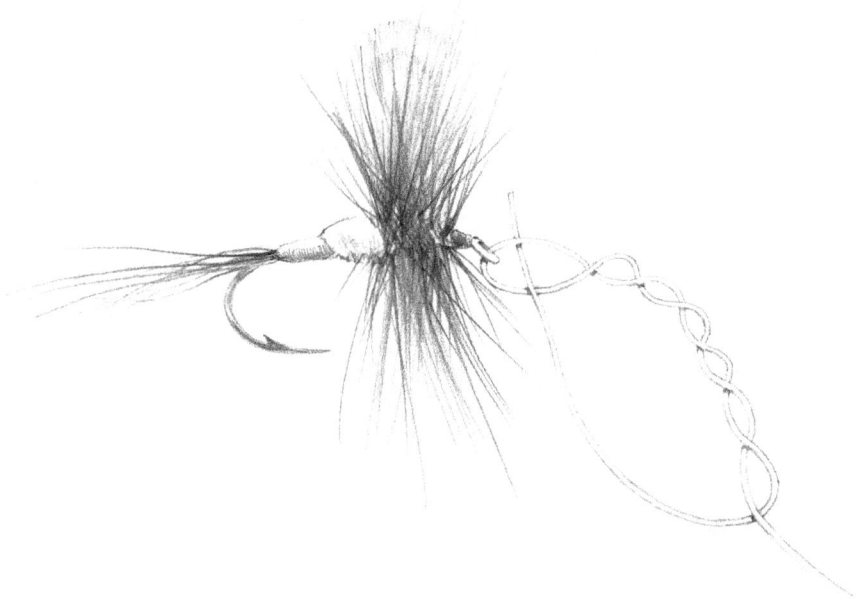

Chapter 20

RAIN, HAIL OR SHINE

One of the most frequently asked questions about fishing is the effect the weather plays in the whole scheme of things. A knowledge of the weather is vital to removing the hit and miss successes we would otherwise experience. There is any number of theories from the scientific to the mystical. Some seem obvious and others far-fetched. The one undoubted truth in this whole business is that the weather is of tremendous importance to the freshwater angler if he or she wants to level the playing field with our speckled friends.

Fishermen often blame the weather for their failures but rarely credit it with their successes. Choice of fly or enormous personal skill rate much more highly with anglers than favourable weather conditions. Of course the opposite is also true where the rain is blamed along with the dreaded southerly or easterly wind that suddenly whipped up and put the fish off the bite. Some people even dislike a full moon or sudden changes in barometric pressure. These are all marvellous excuses when things go wrong and can be the subject of intense discussions at day's end in front of a roaring fire, while you enjoy a hard earned beer or whisky.

From a practical point of view the wind is very important to fly-fishers, as it can be either an asset or a disaster for casting a fly line any reasonable fish catching distance. A strong wind from behind can greatly assist casting, whereas a really strong wind in your face can make presenting a fly almost impossible. Many people hate fishing in the wind, but it can provide great camouflage by ruffling the water surface and it often blows a lot of insects onto the water and this can really get the fish moving. I've heard of people intentionally walking a grassy lakeside bank and getting the grasshoppers in the air and a strong off-shore wind blowing them out onto the lake. I'm not sure if 'berleying' like this is strictly kosher for fly-fishers but it does illustrate a creative use of the wind in very specific circumstances.

Rain can be uncomfortable, but it rarely puts the trout or other freshwater fish off the bite. With good quality wet weather clothing the wind and rain can be thwarted and this leaves us with a ruggedly comforting 'I can cheat the elements' feeling. This means we can largely ignore the weather and get on with the fishing. Comfortable fishing invariably means better results and you can concentrate on what you are doing rather than suffering in silence.

More subtle than the elements of wind and rain are factors like temperature of the air and the water. Really cold water makes the trout and many other species listless or dormant. Water that is too warm can kill fish, because the warmer the water the less dissolved oxygen is present. There is a direct correlation between water temperature and fish activity. This is compounded here in Australia where many of our trout live in marginal environments where there are large daily ranges in the temperature of water in streams and around lake foreshores.

This is where time of day becomes relevant and one of my favourite rules of thumb is to go fishing when it is most comfortable for the angler. In the middle of summer the daytime temperatures can soar and therefore the water around the shallow margins heats up to its highest temperature during the middle of the day. Not comfortable for us and rarely suitable for the fish. The best fishing at this time is very early morning or late evening. Early morning in particular sees the fish feeding in the cooler lake shallows or active in a stream. As the day heats up they retreat to the cooler depths in a lake or shelter in the deeper shady runs and pools in smaller streams. Armed with this knowledge we now know where to look for trout at any time of the day during the warmer months.

Winter time and the shoulder periods of late autumn and early spring are more suited to that old fashioned term 'bankers' hours' where a later arrival is much more appropriate. Frosty mornings often develop into beautiful days. As the water gradually warms the insects start to stir and so do the opportunistic trout. These are great days with a somewhat lazy flavour. A relaxed breakfast with an extra cup of coffee and a good gossip about the prospects of the day ahead is particularly pleasant. This is an unhurried approach when compared to the ridiculously early starts that we love to complain about in summer. Different seasons, different strategies, the early mornings and late evenings are certainly worth the effort. During winter the later starts are positively luxurious!

Light intensity is a factor that significantly affects trout because they do not have eyelids as we do, so they are very sensitive to intense sunlight. On really bright days where the water surface is unruffled they will go down deep or lay up in the shade where possible. This gives us a clue to the trout's whereabouts on very calm sunny days.

Barometric pressure is another variable that some anglers believe affects trout behaviour. The passage of weather fronts across the continent that we see on the nightly news as a series of concentric circles around the letter L or H, are supposedly detected by the trout. This has to do with their swim bladder that allows them to hover in the water. They compensate for the air pressure and the gases in their swim bladder and some anglers say that when the air pressure is low the trout often go deeper in the water and when it is high they prefer shallower water.

When you consider all of these variables it is hard to imagine we could ever catch anything. The reality is that these facets of the weather are just part of the picture and personal determination and appropriate equipment and practice also factor largely in the fish catching equation.

Like all wild animals trout are highly attuned to the weather. To have any chance of catching and releasing these superbly evolved creatures we need to be become more aware and sensitive to the prevailing conditions. Such knowledge will give us a greater appreciation of nature and our reward will therefore be much more than simply outwitting a precious trout or two.

Chapter 21

SINK OR SWIM

Fishing in all its varied forms is almost certainly Australia's largest participant sport. Enormous numbers of Australians fish every weekend and many more fish at least once a month. Look in just about any garage in Australia and you stand a good chance of finding some fishing gear. With such a large participant base it is surprising that we hear so little about fishing in comparison to other sports like cricket, golf and football that seem to dominate our nightly news programs. The answer is probably that these are competitive sports whereas fishing is seen generally as recreational and non-competitive.

The other aspect of fishing that we rarely hear about is the relative dangers involved and the numbers of people drowned every year. If fishing gets a mention on the news it usually relates to the drowning of a rock fisherman and these tragedies play themselves out too frequently around our Australian coastline.

The fact that fly-fishing can also be dangerous was brought home very clearly to me recently when one of my best friends was telling me about a near death experience his father had while fishing the Swampy Plains River below Khancoban Pondage on the western side of the Snowy Mountains. This eighty-one-year-old grazier was spending the weekend with his fishing mates and decided to do a little solo fly-fishing on a river with which he was very familiar. He was wading across a section of rapid water he had waded many times before but this time the current was too strong and he lost his footing.

He found himself being tumbled through the rapids fully dressed in his waders and fishing outfit, then washed into a deep pool where he was fully submerged. He struggled to the surface for air then the force of the water tumbled him through another set of rapids and dumped him in another deep pool where he was pulled under again. Who knows what thoughts were going through his mind as all this was happening, but with great determination he fought his way to the surface and managed to grab the trailing limb of a willow. Holding on for dear life this eighty one year old found the force of the river pulled him in towards the shore.

He hung there for about five minutes and recovered himself both emotionally and physically, at least enough to drag himself up the river bank and then collapse on the grassy verge. When he came to, he found he had lost his hat and his valuable fly boxes from his fly-fishing vest.

His precious rod and reel also seemed lost until he discovered to his great surprise the fly line wrapped around his neck! He carefully pulled it all in and found his rod and reel intact. They had been dragged through the rapids and deep pools with him and their retrieval, like his surviving this frightening incident, was something of a miracle.

This remarkable elderly gentleman survived because he was strong and very determined. His many years on the land had made him fit beyond his years and he was able to grab that willow and hold on for his life. He was also very lucky. Anyone who knows the Swampy would realise the forces at play in this tailrace fishery. Serious quantities of very cold water are released from Khancoban Pondage on a daily basis and this is what supports such a superb fishery downstream. While not an enormous river it is a very powerful one and a real test of wading even in the relatively shallow areas.

The reality is that if you do enough fishing and do enough wading you will eventually succumb to the forces of nature and fall in. Fast flowing high country streams are magnets for fishermen and they provide some of the most exquisite fly-fishing the world over. The cold, clear, fast running water provides an ideal habitat for trout and the slippery rock-studded riverbeds provide relief for the trout from the ever-present forces of the currents.

Fishermen find in many locations with highly vegetated riverbanks it is more efficient to get in and wade to fish the prime spots and in doing so put themselves at varying degrees of risk.

My friend's father with all his experience made several basic errors. He was fishing alone, and particularly at his marvellous age, he should have had a companion nearby. He should perhaps have also treated the river crossing with more respect. Irrespective of age, fishers should plan their route across rapids and if in any doubt should backtrack and find a safer way up or across the stream. Of course this is easier said than done. The next pool beckons and your confidence levels are high. You have fished this water before and feel you know it well…and ninety-nine times out of a hundred we get away with this approach, but sometimes we overstep or take one too many risks.

Falling in can be uncomfortable, painful, embarrassing, expensive, and even legendary in a hilarious way. We all have friends who have a propensity for falling in and this can be very amusing when the situation is not life threatening. I also think as one gets older and less agile the odds of taking a dunking rise exponentially and obviously favour the river and not the angler.

In angling as in life, age and cunning should outwit youthful exuberance every time. Unfortunately when dealing with the forces of nature the young and the fit often have the edge and the older fisherman must rely more on experience and caution. At least that's the theory. The force of a river respects no one, irrespective of age or fly-fishing ability, and we would all do well to try and remember that.

Nowadays with modern technology there are waterproof waders with belts that stop water from entering over the top in any dangerous quantity in the event of a spill, and there are self-inflating fly-fishing jackets that are real lifesavers for people that fish in deep, fast, water. You can also buy or make a useful wading staff and these are very popular with our friends in New Zealand who regularly cope with much bigger rivers than we do. Anyone who fishes from a boat should wear a life jacket or a self-inflating device and should leave the open thigh length waders at home. In fact I believe there is no place for thigh length waders and fast streams because should you fall in and fill the waders it can be very difficult to pull yourself out because of the weight of the water and equally difficult to pull them off if you are being dragged downstream. I've seen one friend in very serious trouble with thigh waders and I don't use them anymore under any circumstances.

Having said all of that, guess who fell in the Thredbo River a few weeks before the close of last season? I had fished hard and had enjoyed a great three days. On my final wade, having negotiated the last difficult fast-flowing section, I was about to step out onto the bank and looked up to see a friend in the last pool, gave him a cheerful wave—and over I went. No reason, no explanation, just a painful shin, a wet watch and the realisation it can happen to anyone, any time. I didn't break my rod and only my clothes and ego were dampened. Thank heavens for that.

Aviators have a saying 'there are old pilots and there are bold pilots but there are no old bold pilots!' Somewhere in there I'm sure there is a message for all us fly-fishers that love to fish and wade in fast-flowing rocky bottomed rivers. Perhaps the fly-fisher's motto should be 'let discretion be the better part of valour'. And if that sounds too grand, what about 'look before you leap'?

One thing is for certain: I hope I'm still out there safely casting a fly on a delightful crystal clear stream with lots of suicidal trout and a couple of good mates when I'm eighty-one, and I hope you are too!

Chapter 22

THE OBSERVANT ANGLER

Part of the charm of fly-fishing revolves around the opportunities we have to fish in some of the most glorious and diverse landscapes around the world. There are times when the scenery almost overpowers the fishing experience. There are also moments when just being there seems to be its own reward. The size of the landscape can take your breath away, as it so often does to me when I visit the North and South Islands of New Zealand. Immense young mountains, still jagged and snow-capped, feed melting snow to create some of the clearest and most perfect trout streams in the world. This sort of scenery is hard to ignore—even the most determined angler could not help but notice such grandeur.

Of course fabulous scenery alone does not catch trout or any other game fish worthy of pursuit with a fly rod. The truly observant angler is someone who has learnt to recognise the multitude of factors that affect fish and consequently our ability to catch them.

Sudden changes in the weather are a perfect example. Sometimes a change of wind direction like the late morning easterly that comes over the Monaro in southern New South Wales immediately stops the fish feeding on the surface. It's a signal to the observant angler that they may as well go home—or try some different location or tactic.

Water temperature is another vital ingredient in catching trout and many other species. If the water level in a stream is low and the weather hot then the chances of trout feeding comfortably are greatly reduced. Trout prefer cold, highly-oxygenated water and, in times of rising water temperatures, the fish go off the feed and look for the coolest part of the stream and wait until the water cools down again late in the afternoon or overnight. Having observed increasing water temperature with the aid of a thermometer an angler could give up fishing, and come back when temperatures are lower, like late in the afternoon or very early in the morning. Alternatively they could target the fish in those shady or deeper cooler areas of a pool or lake where the fish have retreated, by fishing a sinking line to get a fly down to the fish.

Visually locating fish can test even the best angler's powers of observation. Rainbow trout, in particular, are very well camouflaged and in the right conditions can be almost impossible to see. Sometimes it is a matter of looking into deep rocky-bottomed fast running rivers and looking for something out of place. That something might be a moving shadow on the bottom or that telltale blink of white that we see for just a moment when a trout opens and closes its mouth having grabbed a passing insect underwater. Perhaps it's the shape of a tail sticking out from under the shade of a willow or the momentary smooth patch a fish can make when it bulges near the surface to grab a rising nymph in a windblown lake. The more of these little observations an angler is able to make, the better the chances of locating and catching their quarry.

One of the great secrets of observation is to slow down and really look. You cannot hope to see what is really going on in a slow moving pool or towards the tail of the pool unless you are prepared to wait and watch. I know I'm often guilty of moving on too quickly. It is so tempting to fish blind the ten per cent of the water where you know the fish invariably hang out. How much more fun it is to see your quarry and fish visually. This requires patience and time. You need to sit or stand quietly and wait to see if a fish is cruising a beat, or whether it is just rising on station, and then work out what insects are being consumed.

Some people become incredibly adept at spotting fish in both fresh and saltwater. Professional guides who spend a large portion of the year on the water can see things that we mere mortals find unbelievable. I remember one day fishing with my favourite New Zealand South Island guide, Will Spry, and being completely unable to see a fish he had spotted. It was early in my time spent fishing these fabulous waters and I had real trouble in looking through the water, and picking up on shadow or just little things that were different that spelt trout. I was using glasses with polarised lenses but having trouble with light and shade situations. Will said that canting your head from left to right can sometimes help with finding the right focus and getting the glare reduction just right. Hopefully with good quality glasses the perfect spot is with your head upright, otherwise you can end up with a cricked neck. Will had a pair of glasses where he had to cock his head at about 45 degrees—needless to say, he got rid of those quick smart.

In the end we hooked that fish by remote control. Will directed my casts on to target and the rainbow engulfed the dry fly and tore off uncontrollably downstream and snapped me off in a matter of seconds. I couldn't believe such a big fish was invisible to me, and I determined from that point on to get serious about learning to see trout under as many conditions as possible. I'm getting better, but I doubt I'll ever be in the league of the professionals, as they get so much more time on the water practising their skills of observation.

The good news is that over time an angler can build up a vast memory bank of useful observations that may reoccur frequently or just be useful on an odd or very specialised occasion. Indeed there are times when anglers observe something totally uncharacteristic of trout behaviour, like fish rising furiously during the hottest part of the day, or ignoring live grasshoppers being blown onto a lake and only accepting tiny dry flies gently cast to them, while the angler watches in total disbelief. A sort of reverse match the hatch that makes you realise that there are rules, and that there are no fixed rules.

There is one general rule of thumb in fly-fishing that says that ten per cent of the anglers catch ninety per cent of the fish. These anglers are the ones who invariably take their time to observe and assess any fishing situation and come up with a successful solution. A perfect example of this is where the trout are being very selective about what they are eating. This can come about because there is only one particular type of insect hatching from the depths, or one size and colour of land-borne insect being blown onto a river or lake. It is at times like these that observant anglers take the time to identify what the trout are eating and do their best to imitate the size and colour of that particular insect. Even then there are times when matching the hatch is not enough. The successful angler needs to delve deeper and look at the way the insect is actually presenting itself.

I remember a story told to me years ago by my good fishing friend Glen Preece, well-known local Southern Highlands artist (and illustrator of this book) and a very skilful and patient fly-fisherman. It was about a particularly frustrating morning he had while fishing the upper Murrumbidgee River near Adaminaby. It was high summer and the grasshoppers were everywhere. The trout were actively feeding on these hapless windblown insects, and no matter how carefully Glen presented virtually identical imitations of the grasshoppers in both size and colour, the fish ignored them. In frustration Glen eventually drove back into town and asked the man in the tackle shop what he was doing wrong. When Glen explained what fly he was using and how carefully he was presenting it so as not to spook the trout, the man in the tackle shop laughed and said that he needed to slap the fly down as this was the way the grasshoppers were landing in the river. Armed with this advice Glen went straight back to the river where the trout were still busily vacuuming down the windblown grasshoppers. Against all his better instincts he slapped the grasshopper imitation close to the nearest rising trout and was immediately rewarded with a voracious take from a good fish. This exciting fishing continued for a couple of hours until the trout had presumably had their fill of grasshoppers and Glen had caught and released a very satisfying number of these very particular fish!

As a professional artist Glen makes his living by observation, and then rendering what he sees successfully on canvas. Glen had learnt a valuable lesson that day about how observing and identifying the insect was not enough to fool any of those wily trout. As soon as he understood that he had to go further and actually observe the way the grasshoppers were landing in the stream, he was immediately successful. He presented his fly with an aggressive cast and a seductive plop. Now that's what I call the perfect combination of observation and presentation!

Chapter 23

THE MIGHTY TONGARIRO

New Zealand is world renowned as a destination for serious fly-fishers. Lake Taupo is the largest lake in New Zealand and is found in the centre of the North Island about a four and a half hour drive south from Auckland, or a four hour drive north from the country's capital, Wellington.

Lake Taupo is the product of a seriously enormous volcanic explosion about 2,000 years ago that created a lake 40 kilometres long and 30 kilometres wide which covers more than 600 square kilometres. With an average depth of 120 metres and the deepest part being 160 metres, this lake is like an inland ocean. There are numerous rivers that feed into the lake and the fishing in these streams in season can be quite spectacular.

Brown trout from the United Kingdom via Australia and rainbow trout from California were liberated into Lake Taupo in the 1880s and a fishery of mind-boggling proportions evolved. The early catches were phenomenal with one example mentioned by Peter Gould in his comprehensive *The Complete Taupo Fishing Guide* when two anglers in 1911 caught seventy eight trout, with a photograph of the fish laid out in rows, with the lower two rows containing no fish under 15 pounds! The total weight was approximately 870 pounds. In those days there were no catch limits, and sportsmen judged their success by sheer numbers and weight of fish killed. This is of course very much in contrast to attitudes today, but indicative of the quality of the fishery and the fish of the time.

The natural food sources in the lake and rivers could only last for so long, and the average size of fish crashed, so the government instigated a netting program to reduce the numbers of fish and thus allow the remaining ones to grow larger again.

It was shortly after this successful initiative that the Taupo region achieved world acclaim when famous American novelist and fisherman Zane Grey visited the area in 1925. He wrote most enthusiastically about the fabulous trout and the local environment in his book *Tales of the Angler's El Dorado, New Zealand*. He visited New Zealand again several times and stayed for extended periods to write and satisfy his passion for the fabulous fish that run up the major spawning streams that remain open year round like the Waitahanui, Hinemaiaia, Tauranga-Taupo and the most famous of all, the Tongariro.

When the fishery inevitably crashed again in the mid 1930s the government decided to introduce a native smelt from the Rotorua area. They have thrived ever since and provided the essential food source that has made Taupo the extraordinarily successful and consistent fishery it is today. With fish averaging nearly four pounds and the real likelihood of catching both browns and rainbows between 10 pounds and 15 pounds it is no wonder so many anglers from around the world make regular pilgrimages to this year-round fishing destination.

Amidst all this angling splendour flows the mighty Tongariro, which in February 2004 experienced some of the worst floods in its history and saw several of the famously named pools either disappear or be relocated by the incredible power of the floodwaters that roared down into the lake for several days. Fortunately the river has survived this scouring and the fishing during the famous winter spawn run in 2005 was excellent and hasn't looked back since.

The traditional method of wet lining across and downstream is still very effective with sinking lines and large colourful wet flies. In more recent times there has been a growing trend to upstream nymphing with floating lines and strike indicators attached to the end of the fly line. This is followed by a straight ten or twelve foot leader of eight to ten pound breaking strain monofilament or fluorocarbon, a heavily weighted nymph, then a short foot long leader tied to the bend of the nymph with a size 12 or 14 Glo-bug on the point.

This rig can be a little unnerving to cast. It requires a rod in the eight-weight class to cope with both the casting and fighting the large boisterous fresh run rainbows that pour up the fast flowing Tongariro in vast numbers to spawn over the winter months. These fish move quickly up the river whenever there is a period of low pressure weather with overcast skies and rain. They tend to lie in well known runs in pools with marvellous names like The Major Jones, Judges, Cattle Rustlers, Neverfail, Duchess and Old Admirals. These pools are the stuff of legend and need to be fished in the same way as a connoisseur of fine wine might visit a winemaking region and sample the products.

In each of these pools there is a particular part that is recognised as the most productive during the winter spawn run, and anglers line up and fish them in either an upstream or downstream procession depending on the method being used. There is a code of conduct that is applied and this generally works well. The idea being to make a cast or two then move up if you are upstream nymphing, or down a couple of paces if you are fishing with a sinking line across and down the river. This way everyone has a fair chance to fish the most productive parts of these famous pools when there are large numbers of anglers sharing the river. Once you get to the tail or the head of the pool you leave the water and return to the other end and start again. Where anglers practising two different methods come together then it is just a matter of common courtesy to allow one or the other to pass and resume their style. Mostly this works, but as in life, there are always the occasional individuals that want to hog the prime spots and they need to be communicated with courteously to hopefully educate them about sharing the river.

While this style of fishing is not everyone's cup of tea, it is an opportunity to catch significant numbers of large gloriously conditioned fresh run rainbows and browns that you would otherwise be unlikely to catch during the rest of the year. Trophy trout are also caught around the lake foreshores when the smelt are running and it is not uncommon to have a 'picket fence' of anglers at any one of the famous river mouths when the fish are shepherding and smashing into the enormous schools of smelt in against the rocky shore.

There are many highly professional guides available in the towns of Taupo at the northern end of Lake Taupo and Turangi at the southern end of the lake on the banks of the Tongariro. Turangi is a delightfully laid back town where you can wander the streets fully kitted out in your fly-fishing apparel and not get a second glance from the locals. This is a town devoted to trout and everywhere you look there is evidence of how important fishing is to the community. Well known lodges provide comfortable accommodation along the banks of the river and it is easy to catch a fish or two before breakfast right outside your back gate. You never know who you are rubbing shoulders with and polite introductions on the river can lead to fascinating conversations and immediate friendships.

New Zealand is every bit as good today as it was in Zane Grey's time. Granted the average fish size is not as great, but the quality and quantity of fishing available in lakes, rivers and remote streams on both the North and South Islands must still rival anywhere in the world. The very favourable exchange rate between the English pound, the US and Australian dollars and the New Zealand dollar means that all our fly-fishing friends worldwide can hardly afford not to come.

Members of Fly Fishers in the Southern Highlands (FFISH) have been mounting expeditions to this fishery for many years and we have never been disappointed. It is possible to get about on your own on the Tongariro at any time of the year. There are many guides based in Turangi who provide an excellent service year round. They can teach local methods and introduce anglers to their favourite spots which are often tucked away on streams that run through private properties in the hilly country throughout the Taupo region. Alan Simmons is one guide whose services we always enjoy. Alan is well known internationally and has guided many famous anglers including John Goddard and the comedian Billy Connelly.

From a trout fisherman's perspective it is hard to imagine a better place to visit regularly or to retire. The pristine environment and friendly locals make this a place I will return to as long as I can wade a river and cast a fly.

Chapter 24

THE MYSTERY OF LAKES

Ask any fly-fisherman what they think of lake fishing and the answer will probably be a mixture of uncertainty, confusion and probably a fair dollop of awe. Lakes can do that to you. Lakes are invariably big, that's what makes them a lake rather than a pond. They hold an immense amount of water, and by their very nature, are often deep and mysterious.

Fly-fishers who are hypnotised by running water and small streams often find lakes a bit daunting. Having learnt to fish streams and had some success along the way, there comes a time when anglers realise that fishing in lakes offers the chance to catch larger fish, and a whole set of new learning experiences relating to locating these fish come into play. The other advantage of fishing in lakes is that they are open year round. The declared trout streams in New South Wales close over winter from the long weekend in June to the long weekend in October to protect the brown and rainbow trout while they breed. The two alternatives during closed season are to hang up the rod and waders—or fish lakes!

The need to catch a big fish can strike at any time, but the thinking angler will eventually realise that with streams there are often a lot of fish mixed with relatively little water. Lakes on the other hand strike you as a hell of a lot of water between fish. This sort of thinking does nothing for your confidence and needs to be overcome by learning a few tricks of the trade.

Most anglers when faced with fishing a big lake for the first time have no idea what to look for, or where to go. They treat the whole experience as a chuck and chance it affair. The trick is to break the lake into specific areas and analyse what effect the weather is having on the lake and then try to imagine what the trouts' needs are. Trout are never far from food and in a lake most of this occurs in the shallow water near the edges or around submerged islands and weed beds. Deeper water inhibits the penetration of light and weed beds are reliant on sunlight so they can photosynthesise and grow. Most of the insects in a lake live in weed beds or under rocks in the shallow margins of the lake, so this is where you find trout cruising.

Sunglasses with polarised lenses are an essential part of the serious fisherman's tackle. When fish are cruising the lake edges it is vital to be able to see them before they see you. Polarised lenses cut the glare from the water surface and allow the angler to see into the water for quite a distance. This is an enormous advantage for the fly-fisher. He can set an ambush for the cruising trout by carefully casting a fly out well in front of the fish, so as not to spook it.

Wind often plays an important part in the fish locating equation. It also plays a part on angler comfort. A wind blowing onto the lake from behind the angler is particularly helpful to the fly caster whereas a wind blowing onto the shore makes it hard to cast a fly any distance into the wind. If there is an abundance of terrestrial insects like grasshoppers, then the offshore wind blows them onto the lake and the trout soon gather for the feast. If the wind has been constantly blowing onshore then the wave action stirs up the silt in the lake margins and the trout cruise the clear water immediately adjoining this muddy water, looking for disturbed aquatic insects.

Water temperature and time of day also play a part in lake fishing. The old rule of thumb that the best time to fish is when it is most comfortable for you applies equally to streams and lakes. On a hot summer day the fish stay out of the lake shallows and only tend to come in close during the late afternoon and feed throughout the night and for an hour or so after dawn. This is when the water temperatures are at their coolest and the oxygen levels at their highest. The warmest time in winter is in the middle of the day and this is when the insects are most likely to hatch and attract the trout into the shoreline shallows.

A selection of sinking fly lines is essential for the serious lake fisherman whereas a floating line is generally all a stream or small river angler needs. In lake fishing there are many times when an angler cannot see the fish and this means they are feeding down deeper on aquatic insects that are not yet ready to come to the surface to hatch and fly together to breed and complete their life cycle. For this deep fishing the angler needs to get his fly down and work it back gently just above the bottom of the lake from the deeper water into the shallows. The angler fishing from a boat is even more advantaged in that he can move around a lake more readily and cover even more options in his search for trout.

During the daytime the majority of fish move offshore into depths between fifteen and fifty feet. Anglers with a depth sounder can locate these fish and attempt to catch them with super fast sink lines that take the fly down as much as eight inches per second. If you know where the fish are you can do the maths and count down the line as it sinks until you know it is at the depth where the fish are holding. If you are shore based and don't know the depth you just cast out and keep increasing the line depth between retrieves until you hit the bottom or start catching fish.

Lakes are places of great beauty and charm. For the fly-fisherman they offer real opportunities both in terms of the size of fish available, and because they give us the chance to learn new skills and broaden our fly-fishing horizons.

The lakes we stock here in the Southern Highlands are the perfect place to practise our lake fishing techniques when we are not away to the Snowy Mountains or the trophy trout lakes of New Zealand. There is some serious enjoyment and satisfaction to be had when we connect with some of the superb trout that have grown fat yet fight fearlessly in these delightful fisheries we have created. As Roy Hauptberger was heard recently calling out with a whoop of delight in the distance, as he hooked up again towards the end of a spectacular morning at one of our special fisheries: 'I...love...this...Club!' It sounded a little crazy as it floated down the valley but I'm sure we all agree, whether it is on a public or private lake, the feeling is the same. Taking the trouble to learn about lakes and having the courage to fish them can provide soul nourishing moments and memories for a lifetime.

Chapter 25

A FLY-FISHING CLUB

Berrima District Acclimatisation Society (BDAS) was formed many years ago to introduce trout into the Southern Highlands region of New South Wales. It operated very successfully distributing large numbers of brown and rainbow trout that were supplied by NSW Fisheries into various local waterways. These introductions were only moderately successful because of the marginal nature of the area for stocking trout. At an altitude of about 650 metres we are right on the limit of where trout normally survive all season. There are almost always a couple of weeks in high summer where the water temperatures rise just enough to see oxygen levels depleted and this kills off the trout in some of our streams. There were various other initiatives many years ago like building a spawning bed from imported gravel at Wildes Meadow creek which runs into Fitzroy Falls Reservoir. The idea was to encourage the trout that ran up the creek every year to spawn naturally and so augment the fry and fingerlings that were regularly stocked in the reservoir. The success of this initiative is largely unknown because that creek was closed to angling of any kind some short time after the spawning beds were installed. Some would say this was the beginning of the end for BDAS as difficult economic times and changes of governments saw differing attitudes to the introduction of non-native species.

It was also a time of generational change, and the old guard either moved away or passed on to the fly-fishing adventures of the afterlife, leaving the Society with only a small bank account and a handful of earlier members who had any knowledge of the Society's activities before the mid 1980s. For all intents and purposes BDAS was dead.

I moved with my very pregnant wife Julia to the Southern Highlands town of Bowral in 1993 having sold my real estate agency in the Sydney suburb of Castle Hill. We were looking for a change of lifestyle. Little did we know that we were one of the first waves of people who wanted to experience a tree change. Apparently the sea change people went to the coast—but we went to the country—and it's a move we've never regretted. Our daughter Katie was born a month after arriving in Bowral and it's been all action since then.

We met Glen Preece and his wife Victoria through our children at school. Glen was starting to make his mark as an artist and his considerable talents were beginning to become recognised. It was a chance conversation that made us realise we both shared a love of fly-fishing. He introduced me to local physiotherapist Roger Sawtell, and we three started having adventures to the Snowy Mountains and the soon to be drought-ravaged Monaro region of New South Wales. We explored many of the rivers down south and when they started to dry up we began to explore the small streams above Goulburn around Crookwell and Taralga. We had some great times and caught some superb trout in these slow moving creeks but it was not long until these waters were also suffering the effects of the ongoing drought.

It was about this time that Glen mentioned that there had been an active acclimatisation society in the Southern Highlands that had gradually petered out, and that he thought there may even still be an active bank account with some funds that the members had raised largely through the generous donations he had made by way of paintings that had been auctioned.

You can imagine how my ears pricked up when I heard that! A little investigation and with the help of several of our members, in particular local accountant and fellow fly-fishing enthusiast David Brindley, we managed to track down the account and BDAS was reactivated. We opened up communications with NSW Fisheries and re-affiliated with the Council of Southern Districts Angling Clubs (CSDAC)—and the rest as they say is history.

I wrote a regular column on fly-fishing for six years in the highlands lifestyle magazine *Highlife*, and the editor David Smith kindly allowed me to mention at the end of each article that the Berrima District Acclimatisation Society met regularly and the nucleus of our club quickly formed.

As the drought got a stranglehold on the south-eastern corner of Australia it occurred to me that Bowral and the Southern Highlands were not as affected as the other regions because we were still able to stock trout in our local streams and reservoirs with some success. Everywhere else was becoming more and more parched. There were also some significant properties in the area with large dams that were capable of being stocked with trout and the seed of an idea formed. We had been busily stocking fish for the general public with trout supplied by NSW Fisheries for several years. Anyone with a New South Wales fishing licence could access the creeks and rivers in the area and the restricted fishing area at Fitzroy Falls Reservoir. These large dams on the other hand were on private property and again it was Glen who came to the fore and got me thinking when he said his father and his partner lived on a large rural property with a huge dam. He felt his father's partner would be happy to let our club stock the dam and have regular and exclusive access.

Another club meeting was called and a site inspection carried out. The lake was perfect and we realised that the cost of stocking this dam would have to be borne by the members. No fish from public funding could find their way in here, and members understood this clearly. It was decided to start another private club to stock this lake. One of our clever founding members, Ken Street, said we should call the club FFISH, and explained it was an acronym for Fly Fishers in the Southern Highlands. There were about twenty of us all sitting together at the edge of the lake having a quick cuppa and imagining how good this fishery could be. We all looked at him in amazement—and FFISH it was from that very moment.

Over the next few years we made approaches to various landholders and we now have nine private fisheries spread throughout the width and breadth of the Southern Highlands. The stocking of these waterways is entirely funded by members and we stock brown and rainbow trout and native Australian bass in two of the lakes, along with the trout. Membership in FFISH is restricted to fifty members so that none of the fisheries and their owners is ever overwhelmed by members visiting. The annual fees cover the cost of stocking all our lakes and also fund the dollar-for-dollar native fish stocking program which sees us putting about 5,000 bass every year into the decommissioned Welby Water Supply dams at Mittagong.

Today Berrima District Acclimatisation Society incorporates Fly Fishers in the Southern Highlands and runs rather like a golf club with, in our case, two levels of membership: the public component BDAS and the privately funded FFISH group. It continues to be a big success with a flourishing membership and a band of enthusiasts that promote all that is good about fly-fishing. We meet every month of the year except January, and have regular trips away to the Snowies, saltwater venues and New Zealand. We have picnics for all our members at our private fisheries each year so that our BDAS members get to enjoy them and see what we are doing privately in the district. We are fortunate to have many very talented members who produce an excellent newsletter and DVDs of our various adventures. We have talented fly-tyers and one especially talented cane rod maker, Callum Ross. Meetings are always very well attended—we try to regularly have guest speakers and this makes the meetings even more stimulating.

As a property investor, I always say to my wife Julia that I wish our property ventures were as successful as BDAS and FFISH—and she looks at me with a wry smile—she knows that BDAS and FFISH is the best thing I've ever done and never made a dollar from, and it was only achievable because a group of dedicated guys got together with the support of their patient and understanding self styled 'ffishwives' and formulated a plan to benefit fishing in the region both publicly and privately. We are enormously indebted to the lake owners who trust us with their precious lakes and allow us exclusive access. Many friendships have been formed here as well, and it has been the opportunity to introduce our lake owners and their families to fly-fishing that has made the whole initiative even more rewarding.

Starting a fly-fishing club is a tremendously worthwhile exercise. It is a huge amount of work for the dedicated few who form the executive and run the club, but the rewards are enormous. The camaraderie and the chance to introduce new anglers to our special sport make all the effort worthwhile. The pool of knowledge that is available to new fly-fishers is a precious resource and the opportunity to promote fishing in the wider community with the help of NSW Fisheries is a real winner. There are many fishing clubs in Australia and they all play their part in promoting the sport of fishing. BDAS and FFISH are dedicated to fly-fishing and thanks to the enthusiasm and dedication of its members are guaranteed a long and exciting future in the beautiful Southern Highlands of New South Wales.

Chapter 26

CAPTURING THE MOMENT

There are many parts that make up a whole when it comes to enjoying a fly-fishing experience. Good weather, good company, a competent caster with the right fly, and of course a willing fish or two. All these things are important. Sometimes it is even more than these. There are times when solitude and the sounds of nature add that special ingredient. Scenery can often make your day special, especially if the fishing is slow. Catching fish is not critical, but a good day, depending on your personal viewpoint, is often measured by quality rather than the quantity of fish caught.

In the 'good old days' the measure of success was often the number of dead fish in the bag at the end of the day. Such a day was often recorded in a photograph showing a pile of lifeless fish all laid out in a row with a beaming fisherman or two in the foreground. In more recent times the focus has moved to a more conserving approach with catch and release very much in favour with most fly-fishers today. While there is nothing wrong with keeping a fish or two for the table, there is no excuse for keeping everything we catch when we are not reliant on fishing for our survival. The whole idea is to carefully release fish for the future of fishing. This is particularly relevant to trout fishing in small creeks and rivers where population sustainability relies on the mature fish breeding naturally…our fishery biologist friends call this natural recruitment. These large fish are both trophies and breeders. Take one home as a trophy and that is one less fish to ensure continuation of the species.

One aspect of fly-fishing that is growing alongside the concept of catch and release is photography. Some wags call it 'fishography'. Well whatever you call it, carrying a camera is a great way of recording your success without killing the precious fish. The saying that a picture is worth a thousand words is particularly true for fly-fishers. The ability to capture the moment of success in catching and then releasing a fish is available to everyone with a camera and some basic skills.

A good fishing photograph can be a close up of the angler cradling the fish before release. A photograph like this gives you the opportunity to look back on the day and refresh your memory for years to come. To make the most of such a photo opportunity it is important to fill the frame as much as possible. If you have a camera with a flash this is particularly useful in low light conditions or where the sun causes a dark shadow over the angler's face if they are wearing a hat. Under bright sunny conditions you need to use the flash manually and most automatic compact cameras offer this feature. It is amazing what a difference this one technique will make to your photography. The look on a person's face is also worth a thousand words and you can't see this if their face is in shadow. Try it with some family close-ups and see what I mean. Flash is only effective at relatively close range but the simple rule I use is: if in doubt, use the flash.

Action shots in fishing photography are very worthwhile as they convey the excitement of the moment and record the general scene during the struggle. Three or four shots can capture the whole experience from beginning to end. The trick here is to again fill the frame as much as possible and try and keep the sun behind you. Ideally you will want the angler and the fish in the shot. The flexing rod is a bonus if you can get it in without sacrificing too much distance or angle. A fisherman fighting a fish way off in the distance rarely captures the imagination. Always be careful not to get your shadow in the photograph and don't be afraid to snap off several shots as this greatly increases your chance of getting one really great one.

Most fly-fishers carry compact cameras and they are usually more than adequate for the purpose. Enthusiasts or professionals carry much more sophisticated equipment in the form of a single lens reflex (SLR) camera with telephoto lens and various filters. This gear can be very expensive and any camera needs protection if you are like me and take the odd tumble in the stream! Soft camera carrying cases protect against falls but they let the water in and this invariably gets into the camera and puts it out of action. Wrapping your camera in a zip lock sandwich bag provides good protection in a soft nylon pouch where waterproof carry cases are seen as too bulky. Another alternative is a quality waterproof camera that you know takes reasonable shots.

Knowledgeable anglers use polarised lenses in their sunglasses to take the glare off the water and allow them to see the fish. A screw on polarised filter allows the photographer to cut the glare and capture the fish in the water. Professional photographers get up to all sorts of tricks with their specialised knowledge and produce the exceptional shots we see in quality magazines.

With the arrival of the digital era in photography we see unbelievable technology in very compact cameras that even have the ability to take short bursts of video. Digital video cameras allow us to take both stills and quality video footage only dreamed of a few years ago. These images and still photographs can be downloaded to your computer and specialised programs can be used to make your own fishing DVDs, as several clever members of our fishing club do, using the footage we get on our fly-fishing adventures in Australia and New Zealand. This is truly extraordinary progress in the world of photography in such a short time.

Your local camera shop is the place to start your fishography career. They will answer all your questions and sell you the right equipment. When you or a friend gets a trophy trout you will have the option of keeping it or taking some photographs for posterity. If you take the photographic option and release most of the fish you catch, you will be doing us all a favour and at the same time creating a permanent record of your special moments which you can look back on and enjoy forever.

Chapter 27

PHEROMONES AND
THE FAIRER SEX

Somewhere in the history of fly-fishing someone decided that this sport was blokey. A man's recreation, secret men's business, call it what you like—but nothing could be further from the truth.

Miss Georgina Ballantine caught a 64 lb salmon on the River Tay in 1922 and this stands to this day as the biggest salmon taken on rod and line in the United Kingdom. Mrs Clementina Morison holds the record for the largest fly caught salmon, a 61 pounder. These are huge fish and extraordinary records. There are many more examples of women catching more and larger fish than their male counterparts and this is particularly surprising considering the enormous difference in the number of men fishing in comparison to women. If our sport is blokey then it's only in terms of numbers participating, not in terms of success per capita.

How often have we heard of a husband or boyfriend introducing his wife or girlfriend to fishing only to find himself being soundly trounced in the fish catching department? The fact is that women make marvellous fishers and this is nowhere more true than in fly-fishing. Certainly there are far fewer women fishing a fly but they surely make up for this deficiency when the results are reviewed. It would be a fair bet that our women fly-fishers in Australia are equally as successful as their English or American counterparts and presumably for exactly the same reasons.

Why is this so? That's simple: it's the pheromones—at least that is the explanation put forward by the authors of a remarkable book entitled *Salmon & Women—The Feminine Angle* published in the United Kingdom in 1990.

It is well known that sea run salmonids rely on their extraordinary sense of smell and taste to return from several years away at sea to their river of birth and to spawn in exactly the same stream in which they themselves were born. Extraordinary examples of these migrations can be seen among the various species of salmon and steelhead trout that spawn in the rivers of the north-west seaboard of the United States of America. These fish leave their birthplaces and travel to sea and return over a period of several years and the cycle begins again. Scientists also believe that social communication exists between these fish and that this is achieved through the chemical messages of pheromones: hormonal substances given off in scent, usually from the skin, which can also affect the behaviour of animals of other species. Salmon can detect water borne chemical messages to an amazing degree where the smell, for example, of a man's hand can repel fish, whereas a woman's hand apparently does not.

Experiments with fish ladders, a series of increasingly elevated artificial pools linked together that allow fish to swim up and over otherwise impenetrable barriers like weirs and dams, have seen fish stop moving up these ladders when a man puts his hand in the water at the top. A woman can put her hand in the same spot and there is no effect on the fish moving up the ladder. It has even been suggested that male fish may be attracted to a woman's smell. If this is true the female pheromones are a potent force indeed.

Apparently many of the women anglers who were interviewed for this particular book reacted to the suggestion that there might be a scientific explanation for their success with amusement and scepticism. Some apparently thought it was a male conspiracy, bad losers to a man, who were prepared to attribute female superiority in a predominantly masculine sport to a form of witchcraft rather than to skill and dedication. Who could blame these ladies for feeling this way, whether seriously or in humour, when you consider that over ninety per cent of fly-fishers are men, and yet the ladies seem to get such excellent results per capita. You can just see those grumpy old men wringing their hands and looking for any credible excuse to explain getting out-fished by a woman.

For my own part, I believe the reason women do so well is that they are prepared to listen and learn. They show great dedication, and they become engrossed in the sport. They realise that finesse is so much more important than brute force, and they apply their superior close range spatial and observational skills to their advantage. Where men go at fishing like a bull at a gate, women take a more gentle and observational approach. They probably take in more of the scene that the tunnel-visioned men miss. They are not afraid to talk and ask questions (don't we men know about that!) and they invariably act on this information. Apart from all else they persist (don't we men know about that!), and in fishing as in other facets of life, persistence is invariably vital to success.

I've always been surprised that there were not historically a higher proportion of women involved in fly-fishing. I'm equally not surprised that in Europe and America in recent years their numbers are on the increase, and that they continue to get great results and enjoyment from a sport we men have dominated, if only in numbers, for so long.

My cousin Bruce Sidebottom is a keen fly-fisher and we have all sorts of fishing adventures together. Bruce is married to Sue and she is a keen golfer and was a competitive sailor in her younger days. Sue is obviously very sporty and well coordinated. Bruce looked a little nervous when Sue expressed a desire to try casting a fly rod. It was suggested it would be safer for me to give the lesson because we all know you should never try to teach your spouse to drive or ski...or whatever. Sue took to fly-casting like the proverbial duck to water. She listened and did what was asked of her and the results followed immediately. She is the perfect example of a lady fly-fisher. She didn't try to cast into the next county but got right into skilful casting. Bruce is in trouble now because after two lessons she is casting so well that almost every cast is good enough to fool a trout. High country Victoria or New South Wales here they come. Sue just needs to get some casts over some nice riffled water where there is an abundance of eager little trout to snaffle her dry fly and she will be hooked for life.

We haven't hit her with the theory of females and pheromones just yet—but I suspect she will give as good as she gets, and hopefully enjoy casting circles around us as most lady fly-fishers do!

Chapter 28

BOXING DAY TROUT

The concept of fishing on the day after Christmas seems a little strange, especially when you factor in the potential sluggishness one can feel the day after a serious family feast. There is only so much turkey and cranberry sauce you can eat before all thoughts of virtually anything fade away as the digestion process kicks in! Not to mention the potentially dangerous brownie points deficit that could occur with even the suggestion of such an adventure so close to the big day. Boxing Day for many is a time of recovery, not high piscatorial adventure. Fortunately my wife is used to my trout fishing eccentricities and recently, perhaps for once in my life, my brownie points were actually in the black.

I'm still not sure how I wangled it, but I found myself with my friend and local physiotherapist Roger Sawtell on a delightful secret creek less than two hours drive from home. Considering it was Boxing Day it was surprisingly cool in the early morning before the sun got up and soon sent the mercury climbing.

We parked the car in the shade of a particularly large willow and both cast a cautious eye around the valley paddock. We were relieved to see the ever-present cattle with the penchant for chewing rear vision mirrors and licking paintwork with their sandpaper tongues were somewhere else that day. We donned our waders as much for protection from blackberries, snakes and cow pats as for wading, and set off upstream in a very positive frame of mind. We were not to be disappointed.

The first pool was immediately promising with a large trout constantly rising along the far bank and working its way around a strange looking object in the shallow part of the pool. Closer observation and an appalling smell confirmed the object was a recently deceased poll Hereford cow. Now I've heard of fish attracting devices in saltwater fisheries and berleying and the like, but this trout was feeding actively on emerging mayflies and the proximity and smell of the dead cow seemed completely incidental.

Roger was the bravest (or perhaps the least affected by the smell) so he crept into position and with a deft side cast put one of his favourite flies, a size 14 black and peacock spider, three metres in front of the patrolling trout and waited until the fish was close and tweaked the floating line to move the fly ever so slightly upwards in the water column. The fish's reaction was immediate and it surged forward and engulfed the fly without any hesitation. The fight was both spectacular and surreal with the fish jumping several times and leading Roger a merry chase around the cow's carcass and up and down the willow shaded pool before it was finally subdued and safely netted. A nearly four pound brown with spectacular colouring and spots turned out to be the biggest fish of the day. A quick photograph and the beautifully conditioned fish was released to grow even bigger and hopefully sire another generation come June or July when the urge to spawn will outweigh all other instincts.

Pool by pool we worked our way up the creek, taking it in turns to spot for one another and catching and releasing fish until the rising temperature started to take its toll. A rest in a shady spot overlooking a favourite pool was in order. Roger is a master of lightweight camping and trekking so I was not surprised when a tiny gas fired stove appeared from his day pack and he boiled a billy while we ate a delicious ploughman's lunch. As we nourished ourselves we watched in amazement the antics of the brown trout playing out their territorial dominance games around the pool and wondered at their continued activity during the warmer middle part of the day.

It took us a while to reconcile this continued activity, time of day, temperature thing, but we weren't in a rush and a bit of trout spotting from the midday shade of a substantial willow gave us a great opportunity to catch up on our personal lives and family shenanigans and have a second cup of coffee. We finally decided the temperature of the water was the deciding factor as this creek is spring fed from a series of hillside soaks that supply it with a constant source of cold clean water. This enables the local trout population to thrive year round, and most importantly be able to survive those hot daytime summer temperatures up around Crookwell and Taralga in the Southern Tablelands region of New South Wales.

Having assumed the fishing would go quiet until later in the day we found ourselves heading back to the car and then hiking downstream for an unforgettable afternoon of rising trout, bent rods and tight lines. The action was non-stop and two very weary and happy anglers traipsed back to the car just on dark, having experienced what we both agreed was probably one of the best days of fishing we had ever had anywhere in Australia.

The irony of the whole day did not escape us as we drove home that evening. We discussed the irrevocable pull of distant piscatorial pastures that fishermen experience and the enormous number of kilometres we have both travelled over the years in search of trout. Yet here we were on Boxing Day less than a two hour drive from home, having had the time of our lives with trout as numerous and cooperative as one could wish for.

It certainly was a great Christmas present for a couple of hard bitten fly-fishermen and it certainly looked promising for the rest of what was to be a memorable season. The Hereford carcass disappeared but the big brown was still there for a couple more seasons before a long dry spell descended on the south-east of Australia. Let's hope that some of his progeny are still alive and holding out in some of the deeper willow shaded pools downstream. The rains that must surely come and rejuvenate this part of the country we value so highly for its friendly people and its beautiful brown and rainbow trout.

Chapter 29

THE ESSENTIAL GUIDE

In the world of fly-fishing there exists a number of highly experienced and motivated people who make their living from guiding people like you and me in our never ending and impossible quest to catch the perfect fish. These individuals are so passionate about fly-fishing that they commit themselves to a lifestyle that may never give them fame or fortune. They are often described as trout bums and I suspect that most of them would smile wryly and call that a compliment.

This lifestyle choice allows them to do what so many of us can only dream about. They can be on a river somewhere, almost every day of the season, and form friendships with anglers from all around the world. They may not get wealthy, but they are that special type of people who measure wealth in a different way. Their idea of riches is measured more in terms of their ability to be independent, and spend as much time as possible in the environment of their choice. To make ends meet they often tie flies professionally during winter and do other jobs during the off-season. In a word, they are committed.

For many recreational anglers the thought of hiring a guide seems like an expense they would rather not incur. A lot of fly-fishers feel they have sufficient expertise to go it alone. Some anglers treat going fishing unguided as a matter of pride. Each of these attitudes are valid, but the reality is that guides invariably charge reasonable amounts, particularly when you consider that they transport, feed you, and ensure you have a day at one or more of their special spots. They will often provide you with access to private properties that you could not find on your own. Some guides provide canoe or raft trips and others use boats or helicopters. The sky is the limit as they say, depending on your budget.

Guides usually charge much the same for two people as one, and this is a way of making the whole experience more affordable by sharing the costs with a friend. The average guide charges about the same as a competent tradesperson when you look at a day's guiding fee and turn it into an hourly rate. The days are often long, and the guide is responsible for your well-being from the time you are picked up until the time you get back. They provide quality equipment and keep their vehicles in good order to further ensure your safety.

A good guide needs to be many things to many people. I sometimes think they need to be amateur psychologists. Guides are often exceptional anglers but need to be sensitive to the needs of the beginner. Good guides have their egos in check. They certainly need to be in control of any situation without appearing to be overbearing, and they need to know when to offer advice and when to keep quiet. They must have patience in abundance and a sense of humour if things get tricky. Some of the best guides are masters of understatement, and inspire confidence and a feeling of camaraderie while still maintaining a professional relationship throughout the day. Most guides refuse to fish unless the client asks for a demonstration. The whole day should be devoted to the client. The professional guide ensures that the client has the best possible chance of catching fish, and learning some interesting tips or techniques along the way.

A good guide can make the difference between an outstanding trip and one that is fishless. This is particularly so when you are in unfamiliar territory. Any overseas trip is an expensive exercise and local expertise is often critical to success. A day or two with a guide can be a great introduction and an excellent investment when compared to the overall cost of what for many fishers, may be the trip of a lifetime.

Even the most expert of anglers can benefit from a day of guided fishing. The more experienced you are as an angler the more important it is to keep your expectations at a reasonable level. Professional guides will always do their best to meet your needs. With some good communication the guide can find out the sort of fishing you enjoy, and show even the most experienced angler a few new methods and challenges. When you consider the time guides spend annually on the water, and the enormous fount of local knowledge they possess, it becomes even easier to justify the costs involved to ensure your dream trip is successful.

Over the years, members of our fly-fishing club have visited New Zealand many times, both the North and South Islands. We have engaged guides on all these occasions because, for many of our members these adventures represent the trip of a lifetime. We want to ensure the very best chance of success every day we are there. Over the years we have had the same guides in some areas several times, and it is great to catch up and have another adventure together. We have never struck a dud guide yet, and that says volumes about the quality individuals in New Zealand that choose to live the guiding life.

One or two of the guides have been a little eccentric, or have had ways of going about things that are a little different, or not exactly to our liking. Again communication is the answer here. Sometimes it is as simple as their method of operation. We had one South Island guide who liked to prowl ahead to sight fish and would call us up on a walkie-talkie when he found a good fish. This was all rather high tech, but it made us feel left out of the process and abandoned to some extent. We had to explain to him that we liked to sneak around together as a team and have him help us learn to spot the fish ourselves.

Another excellent South Island guide liked to separate his pair of anglers and take one and work with him for an hour then set that angler up on a pool and then get the other angler and go upstream and fish with him for an hour. This was all good in theory but this tended to have the same effect as the walkie-talkie guide in that one angler always felt a little left out. When it was pointed out to this guide that we liked to work as a team and share each other's successes and get photos and video footage, he realised that this was a fun way of fishing and it keeps everyone involved and happy. He now uses this approach with all his clients unless they specifically ask for something different.

One of our North Island guides loved to connect his clients to trophy trout and he would immediately head for Lake Otamangakau near Turangi at the southern end of Lake Taupo. This lake is famous for big browns and rainbows and his favourite method is indicator nymphing with buzzers or small nymphs along and between the weed beds that hug the shore. What he forgot to tell us was that it might take all day to connect with one of these fish and there were no guarantees of even that happening. We had to tell him that we loved the idea of catching a big one, but that we preferred stream fishing in summer and using dry flies fished upstream. We couldn't fault him for his enthusiasm or his ability to stand in one spot in the lake for eight hours watching a strike indicator but we had to explain that wasn't what we wanted to do all day in paradise. He actually fished to and hooked a really big brown one day when he should have been putting us on to a fish, and that rather annoyed us. Now he takes us to the Big O for a morning or afternoon and a stream for the other part of the day. This works well as we rather like the Big O and the surrounding scenery, and if we don't get a big one that's OK, as we have the rest of the day on a stream nearby. He has ended up becoming one of our favourite guides—and he doesn't fish himself anymore!

We have never had a problem guide, the type you can't communicate with. Perhaps it is the nature of the beast—the sort of person who is attracted to guiding is reasonably easy-going and tolerant. I have often asked guides if they ever have difficult customers and how do they cope with them. Invariably the answer is that there are very few problem clients, and that if one is encountered, it is just a matter of gritting one's teeth and making the best of the situation for the day. That's the mark of a professional.

Give a thought to being guided for at least a couple of days on your next trip into unknown territory. Do yourself a favour and rationalise the expense any way you can. This way you will maximise your chances, make a new friend, learn some new tricks and hopefully catch the fish of a lifetime.

Chapter 30

FRIENDSHIPS

Some of the most rewarding moments in fly-fishing are the times spent with friends. People you've got to know through your shared passion for being on or near water, and getting immersed in the world of trout or bass or something salty.

These friendships can be formed through meeting friends of friends, or perhaps through your children's schooling activities. It may be a kindred soul who plucks up the courage to come to their first fly-fishing club meeting, and who gets right into the camaraderie that these little enclaves encourage. Contacts can be made in any number of ways, and it sometimes seems like the legendary Masonic handshake, or just something that is said, that alerts the piscatorial radar of another fly-fishing enthusiast. We are all affected to some extent this way, and the mere mention of fishing can get an immediate response from a like-minded spirit. In fact it can be a lot like a big wily brown trout seeing your well presented dry fly, and coming up and engulfing it.

One of the most interesting aspects of fishing friendships is the diversity of people involved, and the way in which a love for fly-fishing seems, in Australia at least, to transcend class structure, or occupation and wealth. I know in our fly-fishing club we have an incredible range of people all sharing a common passion, and getting along famously. Club meetings are a buzz of chatter and information being shared amongst the members and guests. There are times when it is hard to silence the crowd and start the meeting.

Over a period of time friendships solidify and a common sense of understanding seems to grow to the point where a day's fishing is shared in every sense of the word. Your little triumphs become your friends' little triumphs, and a level of unselfishness develops that is very gratifying. Fishing together, where turns may be taken at each available fish, is my style of fly-fishing, rather than rushing off as individuals and leapfrogging from pool to pool like greyhounds in competition with one another. My nicest days are spent with a friend taking our time and smelling the roses. A team approach where you take turns fishing and spotting the fish can be just as much fun as fishing alone. There are times when a little solitude goes down well, but I prefer sharing a friend's success, and where possible catching it on video or film for future enjoyment. Sometimes being the spotter and seeing the whole operation come together can be just as much fun as fooling the fish yourself. Famous Australian fly-fisherman, the late John Sautelle, wrote evocatively about this very approach. He had a group of special friends with whom he used to fish and share his experiences and develop his theories and techniques in the glorious Monaro and Snowy Mountains region of New South Wales. Many of his stories revolved around a cooperative approach to fly-fishing where they would take it in turns to sneak along a high bank and spot for a mate. He described how he enjoyed seeing the whole operation unfold and the fun they had when the team succeeded.

I remember a day with good friends, Mark Passfield, Roy Hauptberger and Heath James, sight fishing rainbows cruising the edge of the very steep-sided Guthega Pondage. This is a man-made high altitude lake way up on the roof of Australia near the ski resorts of Perisher and Guthega. It was a cold morning and we parked in the tiny village of Guthega and walked down to the Pondage. We split into two groups and headed in opposite directions. Mark was already rigged before me because I was struggling to take my eyes of the glassy surface of the lake. Just as I was beginning to thread the line through the runners, with one eye on the lake I noticed a nice trout cruise into view. We were standing well above the high water mark of the Pondage and the actual water line was several metres below that. It was a great position to see fish and Mark scrambled down to the edge to make a cast. From water level he couldn't see the advancing trout so I had to talk his casts into the zone. The third cast was perfect and the nymph was sinking gently right in line with the trout's path. It was exciting to watch as the nymph kept sinking and immediately the trout saw it he started to angle up in the crystal clear water for the intercept. Mark was calling up for instructions and I was able to tell him what was happening and finally, when to strike. It was nerve-racking for Mark and unbelievably exciting in a visual sense for me. He hooked that fish and just as he was releasing it, and I was snapping off photographs, another cruised in to view. Here was I trying to rig up and Mark was well hooked into his second fish for the morning! He got that one in as well and looked up and said 'Well...where's the next one spotter?' It turned out to be a great day and one we will both remember for the camaraderie and the way he had two on the bank before I'd even been able to tie on a fly.

Friendships can develop quickly or they can take a lifetime. As an angler matures over time and develops different attitudes to fish and fishing, so too can friendships develop where a sense of comfort and trust develops, to a point where your favourite fishing buddies are pretty much on your wavelength, and you on theirs. Expectations that may have got in the way early on are understood or just forgotten. Competitive streaks or different styles of fishing a pool have been modified to suit both friends. True friends have nothing to prove to one another. They just enjoy the day together and whatever it may bring.

Fishing friendships in Australia must look a little strange to outsiders, who are not familiar with our national pastime of sledging, which we all know is not confined to cricket. What can look like an advanced case of two grumpy old men having a go at each other, is really a highly developed form of communication and humour, that actually means the opposite of what is being said. Friends understand this language but it can completely baffle wives and girlfriends or visitors from overseas. A poorly delivered, fish-frightening cast, may be greeted with 'What a great cast!' or 'Gosh that was a great cast—can we see that again?'. The sky is the limit for this kind of fooling around and in fly-fishing there are always a wealth of opportunities for a bit of fun and games.

Some of the fishing stories that friends recount after the event can be equally amusing, and the truth can be stretched mercilessly, depending on the circumstances and the audience. The 'one that got away' is always a winner, and friends can embellish these encounters or play them down to great effect. The test in all this chiacking is whether this good humour brings friends closer together in the recounting, or whether one is offended by the leg pulling. Real friends never put each other down, and this is never more true than when telling stories about each other to a group of friends.

One of my special fishing friends is leading Sydney barrister Peter Tomasetti, SC. Now Pete is recognised as one of the leading practitioners in his field and is certainly not a man to cross when it comes to recounting stories of past fishing exploits. He has an elephantine memory and that special gift of the gab so prized by leading members of his profession. Share a room or a tent with him and the adventure has just begun. He is the sort of guy whose infectious enthusiasm really gets you in—and watch out for all sorts of ingenious practical jokes along the way. Sometimes though it is possible to turn the tables and get a couple back either intentionally or unintentionally.

On a recent winter trip to New Zealand and the Tongariro River, Pete was thrown in at the deep end as he was pretty new to fly-fishing and we had to kit him out in neoprene waders and set him up with appropriate rod, reel, line and flies. With this all organised we headed off for the morning downstream of the Creel Lodge where we were staying for the week. We turned left out of the back gate on the riverfront and headed downstream to fish our way back to the lodge for lunch. We had quite a good morning and came out of the river near where I thought the lodge gate was. We still had a bit of time up our sleeves and said we would fish on a little further before lunch. Pete was finding the neoprenes a bit constricting and said he needed a toilet stop anyway. I said 'Well the lodge is about 100 metres upstream from here—you'll remember the gate—see you there in fifteen minutes'. Pete hurried off looking like he was running out of time. And we dropped back down into the river to fish the last pool. It was only after we climbed back up the river bank that I realised where we were—a hundred metres or so past the back gate! It suddenly occurred to me that Pete would have hurried along looking for the gate when it was in fact only fifty metres or so back before where we first climbed out of the river. We weren't too worried and figured he'd go a couple of hundred metres and double back.

An hour and a half later in he trudged—apparently he walked for a couple of kilometres before he turned around in desperation and found his way back. If you hear him tell the story—as only someone as eloquent as he could—we set him up, and he had to finally pull off his waders because he got so hot walking in them—and how ridiculous he looked walking back in his socks and long johns along the track—and how desperate he was to find a boys room, etc. We were very sympathetic until we started to find our beds short-sheeted and coat hangers in the pillow cases…and the very large rocks in our bags packed to go home were certainly pay back for innocently sending him off on that little walk upriver while he was busting.

At the end of the day, it is the time spent with friends sharing a common passion for fly-fishing that allows us to develop friendships that can last a lifetime. Adventures, legendary behaviour and tall tales and true, all add up to a unique camaraderie. Friendships like this are worth cherishing because they give us the opportunity to share our experiences and grow spiritually, and to develop levels of trust and intimacy that will serve us well in every other part of our lives.

Chapter 31

TWO HANDS ON THE TONGARIRO

There are very few rivers in Australia that compare to the world famous Tongariro which runs into Lake Taupo in the centre of the North Island of New Zealand. This glorious river offers marvellous fishing year round and in particular features an annual spawn run fishery that gives anglers from all over the world the chance to catch splendidly conditioned rainbow trout fresh from the lake. There are sensible bag limits and many of the fish are released. Interestingly the authorities have reduced the size limit in a bid to increase the average size of fish being caught. The Tongariro is a fish factory and Lake Taupo an incredible resource for growing fish on with the schools of whitebait that were introduced early last century to boost the fishery after its initial boom and bust.

My cousin Bruce Sidebottom and very good friend Paul Greethead joined me for a week on the Tongariro in July 2008. We rented a neat little house owned by an enthusiastic lady angler right near the river. It was a Besser block home with a tin roof, and perfectly equipped and decorated for three keen fly-fishers. In fact everything about the place was trouty down to the place mats and pillow covers! We settled in quickly and then did a quick trip to Sporting Life, our favourite fly-fishing shop in Turangi. Jared and the team were as helpful as ever with advice on what was happening and where to go for the best results. We bought some seriously heavy flies that the locals call bombs and the usual assortment of small Glo-bugs and mentioned we were using two-handed rods this trip. This caused a few smiles amongst the staff but they conceded the long rods are a lot of fun (although rarely seen on the river) and that they may be useful in the wind or for casting really long distances. This was exactly what we had in mind… and besides, they say a change is as good as a holiday.

We had equipped ourselves with three two-handed rods—two Sages and a Cortland—bought from the USA on eBay, as no fly-fishing shops seemed to stock these in Australia. We also ordered Rio floating lines to match and a Rio multi-tip line. Paul and Bruce got Jared to make them both a Rio type 6 sinking line to attach to the end of their floating lines and we were prepared for all the types of fishing you do with single-handed rods but this time we had the double-handers and we also had the advantage of being able to do some serious roll casts that could reach right across the river. We assumed the big rods and spaghetti sized floating lines would cheat the wind and we had a couple of wickedly windy days where we'd have struggled to get a line on the water without them. The single-handed guys were working incredibly hard to get a line out and we seemed to be able to cast in any direction with a minimum of effort. They were certainly a winner in adverse conditions.

We weren't sure how the rods would perform as we had never used them on a river before. We had bought a couple of books and the excellent Rio DVD that brilliantly covered all aspects of spey casting. Simon Gawesworth, a professional caster from England who now lives full time in the States, works for Rio and does casting demonstrations around the world. His demonstrations on the DVD are superbly filmed and are a great primer to giving the two-handed rod a go. It certainly helped us get going with these monster fly rods.

We started out by trying to use the rods for upstream nymphing, much as you would a single-handed rod with a straight 10 foot leader of 8 lb Maxima to the bomb and another 18 inch dropper attached to the bend of the bomb hook, then a small Glo-bug attached to the tip. This is a pretty brutal and difficult rig to cast with a single-handed rod but was easy with the double-handed rods. We found casting upstream was a piece of cake, especially in windy conditions and we also used a clip on Glo-bug yarn strike indicator and attached it to the braided loop that joined the leader to the fly line. I felt a little guilty about having such a big gun but it took very little time to get used to the big rods and make some long casts with easy mending and long drag free drifts. The results spoke for themselves as we started to get among a mixture of fresh run and spent rainbow trout.

Having pored endlessly (according to our respective spouses) over the double-handed rod casting DVDs and got our heads around what Dec Hogan and Simon Gawesworth had to say, we also found our steelheading casts coming together. We couldn't resist using the double-handers to do huge conventional overhead casts where the riverbank allowed a back-cast and these went clear across the river in many places and had the locals looking on with interest. I remember an excellent article written by Peter Morse about ten years ago where he and a friend tried double-handed rods for the first time on the Tongariro and also got some condescending looks from the locals. I've seen photographs of renowned New Zealand guide Chappie Chapman playing a trout on a two-hander on the Tongariro out of the open sunroof of a Toyota LandCruiser so I guess these guys have conditioned the locals a little to the use of such rods. Jared from Sporting Life in Turangi told us he had just got a two-hander in for an eighty-plus year old local angler and we couldn't help but cheer when we heard that news. These rods are genuinely easy to cast because they are so light and you have two hands working them. You balance them with a larger and heavier reel to accommodate the much larger fly lines but they are not cumbersome. If balanced correctly they cast like a dream.

From a practical point of view you only need to make one cast at a time unless you are overhead casting. This would appeal to older anglers because you minimise false casting and therefore tire yourself out less. I can see a real market for these rods in New Zealand and to a lesser extent in Australia, although I've read that they are brilliant fun in the surf and have also been put to good use in the north of Australia by enthusiasts that use them off the beaches and from boats in the exciting barramundi, queenfish and giant trevally fisheries.

Once we had given the upstream approach a thorough workout we then changed to our sinking lines and started fishing the more traditional across and downstream approach. I used the same flies as before but shortened the leader to about four feet. Bruce and Paul also shortened their leaders but fished a single olive green or black woolly bugger. This was completely new to us with the big rods and again they worked a treat. The takes were invariably towards the end of the drift and they were savage. It paid to have a little loop between the line hand and the reel and hold the line gently pressed between the finger and top end of the cork grip, with the thumb on top providing the leverage for pressure on the line with the pointing finger. This tended to avoid snapped leaders on the take. We were surprised at the ferocity of these takes and had many good hook-ups and serious battles with those fit Tongariro rainbows.

It must be insane fun using these techniques and rods on the steelhead rivers on the north west coast of America where the fish are enormous and come back from the Pacific Ocean to spawn several times in their lives. Lake Taupo and its tributaries are stocked with fish that came from this region of America and in the early years averaged about twelve pounds. Big double-handed cane and greenheart rods were used in those days and they were as heavy as anything compared to today's lightweight marvels of technology. The anglers of yesteryear must have been strong and determined to cope with the heavier equipment and larger fish.

Paul used a fourteen foot Cortland 9 weight and I used a fourteen foot one inch Sage 7141 which is really an eight or nine weight rod even though it is designated as a 7 weight. Bruce used a twelve foot six inch Sage 8126 which is rated correctly as an 8 weight and it was an absolute delight to use and almost impossible to prise away from him for the occasional cast. Of all three rods I think Bruce's was perfectly scaled to the Tongariro although our two longer and rather beefier rods made light work of any conditions, yet didn't deaden the spectacular fights some of the fresh-run fish put on.

As the week wore on we kept using and enjoying the two-handers to the exclusion of our much loved single-handed rods. We were continually expanding our repertoire of casts, advancing from basic roll casts to the sexy and effective snake roll. The classic spey casts of yesteryear are as effective today as they were when they were invented on the Spey River in Scotland. We managed to work out the single and double spey casts and used them effectively in many situations. High banks that precluded a conventional cast were no match for the roll casting ability of these rods—the steep lushly vegetated banks meant these rods came into their own.

I must say again how useful the DVDs were—we watched them repeatedly and then attempted the casts almost from memory. There are so few rivers in Australia where these big rods would be useful, at least none that I can think of in New South Wales except perhaps the Eucumbene below Providence Portal and possibly parts of the Goulburn in the glorious north-eastern region of Victoria.

On the very last day we decided to rig up the single-handers and frankly they felt like toys. Rods that we have used for years and considered perfect for this indicator nymphing game seemed so light and ineffectual. Of course they are still perfect but the double-handed rods really captured our imaginations and proved to be magnificent tools for such a splendid river. I can't recommend them strongly enough especially to older anglers, and those with the spirit of adventure and experimentation in their souls. Try a double-hander for the fun and challenge of learning a totally new way of fly-fishing and you will see what we mean.

Chapter 32

THE WAITING GAME

While it might sound hard to believe, learning to take your time and becoming more patient and observant are some of fly-fishing's greatest challenges. The most successful fly-fishers are enormously proficient in these skills. They always seem to catch fish when everything looks to be against them. The weather can be lousy, the barometer can be down and the skies leaden. The rain can be trickling off the brims of their well-worn hats and still they are on the job observing the water and looking for some sign of life. One single delicate rise or a subtle bulge in the water surface signals the opportunity for a careful cast that can turn an otherwise fishless day into a triumph.

Many of us have fishing buddies like this, and if we don't, then it pays to find one. These anglers make fine role models because they invariably have a keen sense of the trout and its habitat. Most of all they have that rare combination of patience, persistence and perseverance. The three Ps are an enormous asset for angling, as in life, and it comes as no surprise that anglers with these qualities are invariably successful in their personal and professional lives.

Truly successful anglers take a holistic approach to fly-fishing which starts with ensuring they have the right gear and they keep it in tip-top order. They are also rather self contained. By this I mean well-equipped for whatever the fishing situation demands, so that they are not distracted from the job at hand. They have confidence in their gear and they get on with the business of observing and catching fish. These individuals are the masters of the waiting game.

Anxious or impatient anglers are most likely to be the greyhounds that race from pool to pool if they see no immediate action. Distant pastures always seem greener. These anglers put down more fish than they could ever imagine. At the end of the day they return to find the observant angler has only fished a few pools thoroughly and invariably caught more fish than them—and particularly better quality or trophy fish. I know this for a fact because I used to be a greyhound and had to work very hard to get my type A angling personality under control. My therapist was my very good friend Glen Preece who is the perfect example of an observant angler. I'm sure Glen learned his powers of both observation and patience during his training as an artist and he has certainly transferred these skills to his fly-fishing for trout in some of the secret creeks in our region. Fishing with

Glen certainly alerted me to the need to slow down and to do the piscatorial equivalent of smelling the roses.

Without doubt the most exciting part of the waiting game is the opportunity it affords for visual fishing. A quiet approach to a pool allows time to really see what is going on in and around the trout's world. Sunglasses with polarised lens and a broad-brimmed hat or a peaked cap help us see into the water, and with a little patience and a well chosen place for observing the pool the action rarely takes long to unfold.

The closer we can get to a pool the better in terms of observation. One pool on a favourite secret creek of mine has a large willow that allows us to get into its shade right on the edge of the pool and provides a brilliant spot for seeing without being seen, as long as we keep still.

It was in this very spot that my friend, Southern Highlands real estate agent Ian 'Stormy' Rayner caught his first trout on the fly. Having got Stormy organised with his gear, tied on a new leader and attached a size 16 Pheasant Tail Nymph, we both headed upstream to my favourite pool.

As we approached we gave the pool a wide berth and came in crouching from the side so the fish wouldn't see our approach. We carefully climbed the barbed wire fence beside the pool and crept into the shade of the willow to sit and observe the pool and its inhabitants. We barely had time to talk about the waiting game when a good sized brown trout cruised casually into view. Stormy was having trouble seeing him until he got the idea of what to look for and once he spotted him he was in business seeing fish for the rest of the day. I suggested taking our time and just watching this fish as it purposefully picked nymphs from between the rocks completely oblivious to us sitting just above him and barely a rod length away. It is an incredible experience being so close to a wild creature that has such strongly developed senses and is so quick to escape at the slightest hint of danger.

We watched him for about five minutes as he patrolled a beat in our tail end of the pool until Stormy spotted an even larger fish as it swum into view. We'd played the waiting game long enough—this fish was just too tempting—now it was time for action. The only cast possible from our concealed position was a bow-and-arrow cast which is extremely useful in really close quarters or amongst the undergrowth where other casts are impossible. This fish provided the perfect opportunity to demonstrate the cast to Stormy.

We waited until the fish was quartering away from us so that we would be in its blind spot and I carefully stuck the rod out towards the fish with the fly pinched between my thumb and forefinger. I had about ten feet of line beyond the rod tip which was mostly tapered nylon leader. I pulled back on the line and aimed the fly just in front and to the side of the fish. I released the fly and it landed close to where I wanted it. As the fly penetrated the surface of the water the trout twitched in recognition of something landing. What an incredible sight—and only visible because we were so close to the trout. The sensitive lateral line that runs along the trout's flank had done its job and alerted the trout to the tiny change the nymph landing made to its nearby environment! It was just breathtaking watching his reaction at such close quarters. The tiny nymph started to sink slowly and the trout casually veered to the left, hesitated for a moment, then inhaled the fly just before it reached the bottom. Stormy saw the white flash as the fish's mouth opened then closed. I talked him through the whole operation and lifted the rod when I saw the trout's mouth close—then all hell broke loose.

I immediately handed the rod to Stormy ignoring his protests and offered up a little prayer. The fish was even larger than we thought as refraction makes them look shorter and narrower two or three feet under water. For a newcomer, Stormy did a great job of keeping the pressure on while the fish cavorted around the pool and we soon had the beautifully conditioned brown to hand and then released after we had quickly admired its superb spots and caramel coloured stomach.

Stormy had his first trout albeit with a little help, and within half an hour or so of resting the pool he used the same technique to hook his own trout. It was a magic day and the look on Stormy's face said it all. The waiting game at its very best—another angler hooked and ready to start the lifelong apprenticeship and never ending learning curve that is fly-fishing.

Chapter 33

THE NAKED NYMPHER

Sometimes in fly-fishing something happens that you don't witness yourself but sincerely wish you had. Sometimes it is so legendary or improbable, or just simply unbelievable, that only the word of the individual or their fishing partner can verify that it really happened. Whether the story is embellished or just presented factually, is a matter for the individual doing the retelling. Trust becomes important here, and a photograph or two, or perhaps a short bit of video, can help to verify the story. We've all heard that a picture paints a thousand words and that a photograph cannot lie, at least that's how it used to be, until we invented computers and along came Photoshop. Now it is possible to make a wrinkly eighty-five year old granny look like a gorgeous twenty-five year old again. Trout that never grow beyond 20 lbs are suddenly longer than the angler's outstretched arms and look three times that size. Fortunately my scrupulously honest cousin Bruce was along on this particular adventure with his digital SLR, got the images, recounted the story, and the truth became self-evident.

Lake Rotoaira is a substantial elevated lake that nestles between Mt Tongariro and Mt Pihanga, just above and south-west of the township of Turangi. It is almost exactly in the centre of the North Island of New Zealand. Turangi itself is famous for being on the banks of the legendary Tongariro River just upstream from where it runs into the southern end of the enormous Lake Taupo. There can't be many better places in the world of fly-fishing that combine such magnificent scenery and trophy trout all year round. It was into this idyllic environment in February 2004, that twelve members of our fly-fishing club arrived for a week in paradise.

We could see the Tongariro was up slightly when we drove over the highway bridge into Turangi just before dark. All that first night the rain beat down constantly on the roof of the lodge, and in the morning a record flood greeted us. Locals were walking around carrying five and six pound trout that they found at first light in the flooded streets. The deck of the road bridge was just above the rampaging pumice filled river. Huge mature trees that had been ripped from the river bank, were stuck firmly against the upstream side of the bridge. This caused the locals and emergency workers great concern. With the force of the river and the enormous resistance caused by the stuck trees they were worried they may lose the bridge. They were nearly as concerned as the twelve anglers who had arrived from Australia the night before, and who were wondering where in this disaster area we could fish! Our local guide Alan Simmons kept us calm, and said he and his guides would work something out. We should take the first day off, let things settle, and wait and see what the next day brought.

One of the guides, who evidently didn't want to lose a day's guiding, said he would still go out if anyone was interested. My cousin Bruce and another of our special fly-fishers who we will give the pseudonym 'Pete' for reasons that will become obvious, said they'd be in it, and off they went. The rest of us heeded Al's advice and had an extraordinary day sightseeing. We realised in a perverse kind of way that while we were not fishing, we were at least witnessing history, as the river scoured its bed and famous pools disappeared or were rearranged and new ones created.

At the end of the day we all gathered for a whisky or two before dinner and awaited the arrival of Bruce and Pete. When they staggered in looking slightly sheepish and with the guide's face a mixture of amazement, bemusement and disbelief, we wondered what had happened. It had to be something pretty special to have such an obvious effect on three seasoned anglers.

Now the previously mentioned Lake Rotoaira is a natural lake and is one of the few privately owned lakes in New Zealand, and requires a separate licence and permission to fish from the Maori landowners' association. It is a natural lake but it has been considerably modified for hydro-electric purposes and it has a very attractive weed fringed shoreline. It has a large number of healthy rainbow trout, and this is where the boys and the guide went that day. It was really one of the few places in the region that would have been fishable, and they made the most of it.

The guide parked at the end of a small peninsula and they got into their waders and assembled their rods. They marvelled at the size and views of the surrounding mountains, and were amazed at the constant noise being made by the thousands of swans that inhabit the lake. The guide led the way, and they waded out knee deep along a submerged man made wall for about a hundred metres. Both Bruce and Pete fished a moderately weighted nymph on a leader the length of their rod with a strike indicator where the leader joined the fly line. They cast into a current that flowed knee deep across the wall when the water was being moved through the hydro system. It was a magnificent spot and the trout were feeding actively while the water was moving. Both boys were getting among them until Pete hooked a particularly nice one that gave him a merry fight. It ended up lodging itself in amongst the rocks below his feet, at the base of the submerged wall.

The guide said 'Don't worry…just break it off…there are plenty more we he came from!' Pete didn't seem to like this idea. Bruce suggested trying to let the line go slack and see if the fish swam out by itself. They tried strumming on a tight line, letting the line go slack, and pulling from all directions with no luck. At this Pete said to the guide 'Hold my rod, I'm going back to the shore to strip and I'll dive down and free it'. The guide said 'You are joking aren't you?' Pete said 'No, I won't be long' and headed off for the shore. The guide looked at Bruce and said 'He is joking isn't he?' and Bruce said 'I don't think so!'

Just as Pete got to the shore a car pulled up, and an elderly Italian couple got out and started admiring the incredible scenery. Pete said a polite hello, and explained he was fishing with the other men out in the lake and had caught a fish which was stuck deep amongst the rocks. The Italian couple spoke English and seemed to understand exactly what he was saying. When Pete said he would be taking off all his clothes and going to swim down and free the trout, the Italian lady looked very interested indeed. On hearing this, and realising Pete was serious, her husband promptly bundled his wife into the hire car, said a quick 'arrivederci' and drove off at great speed!

Pete got out of his waders and all his clothes, put his wading boots back on, and then waded back out. This must have been quite a sight for Bruce and the guide who were apparently still in a state of disbelief. Pete slipped into the cold water and took hold of the line, collected his thoughts, then ducked below the surface and swam down and somehow freed the fish. As if that wasn't enough, he then swam back onto the wall, and stark naked (apart from his boots) took the rod and finished the fight. He lifted the trout up for several photographs, and then gently released it. He then went back to the shore, dried himself, got dressed, put his waders back on, and then returned to the fishing as though nothing unusual had happened.

It is hard to describe the effect the recounting of this incident had on the rest of the guys back at the lodge that evening. The guide confirmed Bruce's story and Pete admitted it was true. There was a bit of a pregnant pause as we all looked a little incredulous and disbelieving for a moment, then we all laughed and laughed. I think we all now have a new found admiration for our special friend.

The guide will never forget the incident as long as he lives—at least that was what was conveyed by the look on his face. Bruce and the legendary angler, now fondly known as 'the naked nympher', huddled together with the digital camera and edited out all the photos that 'needed editing'. The end result was a fabulous photograph of a dripping angler with a slightly cheeky look on his face and a very nice rainbow trout draped strategically, and just barely covering his crown jewels! Thank heavens the water was cold.

Catch and release is something we all like to do most of the time in a fishery like this. Large trout should have the opportunity to be caught more than once. In a river they should be released so that they can breed and pass on their genes for future generations. The concept of catch, *rescue* and release is now something Pete has forced us to get our heads around. I'm not sure how many of us will be brave enough to embrace this new trend, if ever the occasion arrives—at least not in the company of other anglers, especially those with cameras and word processors. It may be my imagination, and I don't mean to impose human emotions on a fish, but the stubborn trout in the photograph that was responsible for the creation of this angling legend, seems to have a slightly confused and disbelieving look on its face...and frankly, who would blame it!

Chapter 34

THE WILD RUAKITURI

New Zealand never ceases to amaze me with the incredible opportunities it offers for the fit fly-fisherman to access on foot unspoilt waters like the legendary Ruakituri River. Located in the eastern region of the North Island, this special river rises in the mountainous Urewera forests and has a reputation as a trophy rainbow trout fishery. As it runs through a national park there are no helicopter fly-in trips, and this is something of a relief to local and visiting international anglers that take the trouble to make the hike into this pristine fishery.

Below the falls, the Ruakituri is an excellent mixed fishery where it runs through largely cleared rural land. Excellent browns and rainbows are available to the competent angler in a variety of waters all surrounded by superb views and the feeling of bigness for which New Zealand is so famous. There are apparently some trophy sized trout in these downstream sections, but patience and permission for access are needed, and a good dollop of local knowledge goes a long way to catching the largest fish in the lower reaches.

Not a huge amount has been written about this river in recent years. I found some references to it in books on fly-fishing by well known and credentialed New Zealand authors. Sometimes what was not said seemed more tantalising than what was said. I did some research on the internet and found out quite a bit more to whet the appetite.

On an historic note, the Ruakituri Valley and the river were the scene in the mid 1860s of a series of battles during the Maori Wars. The local chieftain, Te Kooti, led a group of Maori who fought tenaciously to protect their lands. Colonel Whitmore led one hundred and forty infantrymen in a chase up the valley and through various river crossings swollen by melting snow, dragging their artillery pieces and dwindling supplies. Te Kooti and his men taunted and tempted the troops with various small skirmishes further and further up the valley into the densely timbered country and finally ambushed them, inflicting serious casualties before forcing their opponents retreat and escaping themselves, even though Te Kooti had been shot in the foot. Legendary stuff to be sure and something to think about as we headed up the same valley all these years later.

Imagine my surprise (horror) when the Spring 2007 edition of that superb Australian fly-fishing publication *FlyLife* arrived in the post box, just a couple days before we were due to leave, with a great article by Greg French thoroughly describing the Ruakituri and its various and exciting fishing options. I didn't let this exposure deter me, except for a whispered 'Oh bugger'. I made the most of the chance to trek in there with my cousin Bruce Sidebottom and friend Paul Greethead, who had been there twice before. Paul got us all fired up and mentally prepared for the arduous walk in, with stories and photographs of superb rainbow trout from his previous visits. If there is anyone keener than Paul on trout fishing adventures and thoroughly researching them, I'm yet to meet him. He pores through books and buys every topographic map he can lay his hands on. The internet gets a thorough workover, and all his research is kept in a little notebook in small but legible writing.

This trip began with enough frequent flyer points to fund the flights and an overnight stay in Auckland, where we caught up with Bruce who had flown in from Melbourne. Paul and I landed just after midnight and found our way to the motel near the airport by 1.00 am New Zealand time. You don't tend to notice the two hour difference between New Zealand and the east coast of Australia until you land at midnight and then have to back up and catch a local flight again early that same morning. What with catching up and having a good gossip, we barely got a couple of hours sleep, but the alarm clock rang and after a few mumbles and grumbles the excitement factor cut in and away we went. We caught an internal flight to Napier, and picked up our hire car at the airport for the four hour drive to the top end of Papuni Station where, with permission, you leave your car and head off for the serious walk to the falls.

With the timing of our arrival at the Station mid afternoon, we decided not to attempt the steep haul up to the falls that first day. We caught a couple of nice browns as we zigzagged with our heavily laden packs up the river. We camped in a delightful spot above a huge pool, not far downstream from where we would take the track up the ridge. We thought a little on the bravery and tenacity of Te Kooti and his people and wondered whether we were somewhere close to that historic ambush site. We were very grateful to catch up on the sleep lost from the night before, and I didn't even hear Bruce snore—not even once!

The next morning we fortified ourselves with a good breakfast then packed up camp and set out for the steep climb and long traverse to get to the camp site above the falls. What looked relatively simple on the large scale topographical map was in fact a serious hike, and it was a genuine challenge for Bruce and I, as we were not as fit as Paul. As fifty-plus-year-olds, we were soon made aware of our less than ideal fitness levels, but with patience, and a couple of rests, we made it to the top of the ridge and soon looked down on the falls. Just as we thought we were just about there, the marked trail led away from the falls and led us down into another creek-line for a rest and a much needed drink. Bruce managed to get his digital camera out and get some of his famous nature shots of running water and moss covered logs—then we had to drag him away, and struggle uphill again to follow the track and reach a contour that allowed us to traverse the distance remaining to our campsite. Thank heavens we had spent a few weeks walking and cycling at home to get ourselves ready for the big trek. Note to self: even more pre-trip walking and cycling next time!

Some time into the latter part of the trek I was feeling tired and a bit discouraged because we seemed to be walking for so long away from our destination. You know, the 'so close but yet so far' feeling. I made the mistake of carrying my net on the outside of my pack and it started catching on everything available. I threw what Paul called a quick hissy fit and then felt the frustration subside. I can't really remember the details, it was all over so quickly. I do remember saying a couple of choice words and ripping the net from the offending branch, and that was that. I don't think I stamped on the ground or anything petulant like that. Fortunately the net wasn't damaged. It can be interesting to see the reactions of your friends and particularly your own, to adversity or perceived difficulties. We had a good laugh and mutually agreed that I was a big wimp or sooky boy or something like that, and then trudged gratefully down the last kilometre or so to our campsite above the falls. What a relief to finally be there. A lesson was learned, and on the way out three days later the net was safely inside the pack and there were no further tangles or frustrations or dummy spitting!

The track was well marked with faded orange tags on trees just as Paul remembered, but on a couple of occasions we got confused by wild game tracks, so circled back to find the right path. This is certainly not country you would want to get lost in, and a cautious and observant approach is necessary. There was no sign of wildlife except for the trails made by deer and the ground dug up by wild pigs. In fact it was eerily quiet. We speculated as we walked about how dangerous these wild boars might be if we bumped into one on his own turf, but concluded that without snakes and spiders in New Zealand, that was a pretty fair trade-off. We would keep the food in the tents and try not to attract the pigs to our camp site.

On arrival, the weather wasn't looking too kind, so we immediately set up our tents and strung a fly between the trees to shelter under by the well used fire pit. Rods were assembled in double quick time, and we headed off for a quick look at the river before dark. The Ruakituri looked great with its deep green runs and large wet boulders. It was everything Paul had promised. We could just imagine those monster rainbows nestled in the lee and feeding voraciously on the various insects being swept down between the slippery rocks, and getting fatter by the minute. We had a few casts and did a few nice drifts, but no action, so we headed back to camp and collected a decent pile of firewood and set about getting a good fire going. This was no easy task as the wood was damp and dry kindling very scarce.

As the evening progressed the rain settled in, and we sat gratefully under the tarp in our lightweight camp chairs and ate upmarket dehydrated meals optioned up with rice and couscous. We had a couple of small whiskies each from the duty free 1.25 litre bottle that Bruce and I decided would certainly be worthwhile Paul carrying in. The lightweight tarp was a blessing and we slept like logs in our tiny tents. We did have one cheeky nocturnal visitor in the shape of a large grey puff ball of a possum that we shooed away and who finally got the message when we started lobbing bits of firewood in his direction. He got even by scarpering around the camp and bumping the tents each night, but by that late hour we were invariably out like lights.

Everything had to be carried in on this trip so we were very mindful of weight as we had airline restrictions, and then it was packs on our backs, up that cruel climb to the falls. Anything non-essential had been pared away and left at home or in the hire car. I'd even considered leaving the net, but it did come in handy for quickly landing the magnificent rainbows and weighing them before release. I have friends who refuse to use nets and say they aren't necessary, but they always take a lot longer to get the fish to hand and then release them. I think it is important get a trout in as quickly as possible and then release it straight away to minimise stress and maximise its chance of survival. These Ruakituri rainbows tested that theory a bit as they were probably the hardest fighting trout I've ever caught, but I still think the concept holds good. Get them in quickly, take a photograph or two, weigh them, and then get them back in the water where they belong. Oh and another thing: when you hold them, make sure you keep them in the water as much as possible and let them keep their gills working by keeping your hands clear of their head.

The annual rainfall and melting snow in this river catchment must be considerable because above the falls the whole landscape was wet, dense, steep-sided, and in places covered with impenetrable forest. I kept thinking about those infantrymen trying to move through this sort of country after Te Kooti and his men, who of course knew this locale like the back of their hands. There are all sorts of tree ferns and lichens on trees and rocks. In the overcast conditions we experienced for our three days above the Waitangi Falls the river landscape was eternally wet and cool but still inviting as any wild river is. It must be magnificent on a sunny day. The river was up enough to limit our ability to get very far upstream, so we had to satisfy ourselves with what is logically the hardest fished stretches above the camp site. We had a great time, and although the wading was pretty treacherous with the slippery streamed rocks, we caught several lovely rainbows that fought like fury and were in splendid condition. One can only imagine what the fishing must be like later in the season and further upstream in the less visited kilometres when the river is at a safer level for wading.

On the second night, after a hearty meal, we talked until all hours, then I suddenly felt desperately tired. Bruce was also fading a little, so we decided to call it a night and crawl into our tiny two man tent. I climbed into my sleeping bag, and just as my head hit the pillow Bruce said 'Take a look at these photos Paulo' as he fiddled with his digital camera in the pitch black. I tried to feign interest but was having terrible trouble keeping my eyes open, let alone concentrating on his brilliant images of river and trout and keen fishermen. I really struggled to stay awake, and just mumbled encouragement for as long as I could (all of about 30 seconds) as my eyes were rolling, and then I slipped away into the deepest sleep while Bruce was saying 'and wasn't this one a beauty…and do you remember that… hey Paulo are you awake?…hmmmm'. In the morning he gave me a good ribbing about it over breakfast. Paul said he was grateful he was in his own one man tent, and didn't have to be involved in late night picture shows with one over-enthusiastic photographer.

The fishing was good despite the weather. It was early in the season and we drifted two nymph rigs as we would on the Tongariro but not as heavily weighted. We swapped the traditional Glo-bug for a lightly weighted Hare and Copper or Hares Ear Nymph with a heavier version of the same to get the target fly down deep in the swirling currents. This rig was very effective as the fish were obviously down on the bottom with the low pressure system dominating the weather. We saw no rises but got some lovely rainbows including one on Bruce's last cast for the trip in a really inviting, deep section of the pool just above the camp site. This rainbow gave Bruce an almighty work-out up and down and around the boulders but eventually succumbed to the relentless pressure Bruce kept her under. Only afterwards did he say he was shaking like a leaf, back aching, and sure the trout had the upper hand. It was probably the most serious test of 6 lb Maxima I've ever seen! The end result was the best trout of the trip, an absolutely magnificent near seven pound rainbow that was quickly released to fight another day. The look on Bruce's face said it all. My New Zealand friends would have said it was a 'cracker'! It could only have been better had it been caught on a big dry fly—something like a size 8 Simmons Attractor or a large Stimulator impersonating a cicada during lower summer flows— next time perhaps.

The trek out was much easier than the one in, and we did it in a big half day. Heartbreak Ridge was a delight going down! No dummy spits from yours truly, and the weather finally broke with mixed cloud and sun which only served to highlight the superb mountains and valley walls. We had to backtrack and climb one very steep hill when we found the river unsafe to cross, and at one point we were a little nervous, as we were clinging to the hillside like mountain goats but with the disadvantage of large, heavy ungainly packs on our backs. Still, nothing ventured nothing gained—and that pretty well summed up this amazing experience. If it was always easy then the rewards would not be the same. Difficult access usually means less pressure on the resource, and the Ruakituri is a very precious resource indeed.

We hope to get back one day, and find it just as wild and unspoiled as we left it. It was a tough trip and certainly not for the unfit or faint-hearted. Weather permitting, we will try to get further upstream and see how our efforts are rewarded. It is a credit to all those previous visitors over the years that either burned and buried or packed out their rubbish, as we saw no sign of litter or excessive pressure on the river. New Zealand's wilderness rivers are definitely worth the effort, and provide you with memories to last a lifetime. The Ruakituri may not be a secret any more, but for many it may as well be. For the adventurous angler prepared to put in the effort and walk and climb for quite a few challenging kilometres, it is certainly worth the effort. Long may it and its rainbows run wild and free, and provide the special memories for other serious anglers that it did for us.

Chapter 35

COMPETITIVE FLY-FISHING

If you really want to throw a spanner in the works and get fly-fishers wound up then just mention fly-fishing competitions and whether they are good for our sport. This is a serious conversation starter around a campfire and is guaranteed to polarise those involved into two groups: the ones that tolerate or enjoy competition, and those that think it is the very antithesis of the joy of fly-fishing.

Competitive angling is present in every form of fishing, but it is fly-fishing that seems to best illustrate the benefits and pitfalls that competitions can provide.

Purists say that fly-fishing is about communing with nature and that one should not even compete with the fish let alone other anglers. This is a very persuasive argument because the whole point of getting into fly-fishing as a sport is to gain a greater understanding of nature and enjoy the quiet splendour of stalking wary fish in their special environments. Occasionally fooling them into accepting your imitation of an aquatic or terrestrial life form is an added bonus.

In a typical fly-fishing competition, the angler enjoys the pressure of being allocated a small stretch of river or a boat and boating partner on a lake for a period of three hours. They know that they have to catch at least one trout of legal size to avoid the dreaded 'blank' which earns a penalty point for the angler in that session. In a system where the winner is the person with the least number of points over four three-hour sessions, a blank is almost certain defeat. The person who does best in their session gets one point and the person who comes second gets two points and so it goes until you get to the people who blanked. If there are eighty people competing and twenty in your session then the people that blank get 20 points! This is pressure at its worst if you are the sort of person who goes fishing to relax. It is however very exciting if you are a competent angler who enjoys the challenge of pitting yourself against the elements and pride yourself on your ability to catch at least one fish per session while abiding by a set of rules that are designed to put every competitor on a level playing field.

The purist would of course say that any form of competition that pits man against fish or man against man with numbers of fish as the measure of success is vulgar and inappropriate. This too is an excellent argument in terms of the recreational fishing experience. A fly-fishing idealist would generally prefer to fish alone or with a friend who shares similar values. The idea of fishing as recreation is that there are no limits imposed upon the angler except those that he imposes upon himself. Time in fishing is irrelevant except where other obligations pose a time limit. The maximum number of fish kept is regulated by state fishing law, as is their minimum size. Most recreational anglers take only what they need and many return everything they catch.

Competitive anglers also practice catch and release as all fish are measured and released immediately to ensure their survival. In recent times the statistics gained in competitions are being shared with bodies like NSW Fisheries and provide important information on survival and growth rates of the fish and what future stocking numbers should be implemented in New South Wales.

When the World Fly-fishing Championships were held at Jindabyne in 1999 there was some emotional discussion in Australian angling magazines regarding the nature of competitive versus recreational fishing. The general consensus was that it was a good opportunity for anglers from around the world to get together and share information about fish and fisheries and the latest technology in fishing equipment and accessories.

Every angler is attracted to fly-fishing for different reasons. For some it is the imagery of the languid casting and the beautiful environments our game fish inhabit. For others it is an extension of other angling methods where the never-ending learning curve offered in fly-fishing offers a special physical and intellectual challenge. The competitive angler sees it as a chance to hone his skills and use them to compete within a small elite group of fly-fishers that thrive on pressure and who often contribute to the technological advancement of fly-fishing around the world.

From a selfish point of view, I like to compete in the occasional competition just so that I can share two boat sessions with two excellent anglers and invariably learn lots of interesting tips on how to best fish from boats on lakes. Most competition anglers I know are very generous with their time and information and if you are fishing in an Australian Fly-Fishing Championship it is quite likely that you will be partnered with a couple of the best anglers our country has to offer.

For me, competition angling is just another excuse to go fishing. I would only find it spoiled the experience of fly-fishing if I was partnered with someone who was a bad sport or who took the whole business too seriously. Fortunately this hasn't happened so far in the few competitions I've participated in. There is certainly pressure in competitive fishing but only as much as you impose on yourself. You still find yourself enjoying the ambience of river and lake fishing, while the constraints of time and competition rules pale into insignificance when compared with the opportunities for learning new techniques and making new friends amongst some of the most competent Australian and international fly-fishers.

Chapter 36

THE OLD BRONZE BATTLER

When we think of fly-fishing we mostly think of crystal clear streams and the superb trout that inhabit them. There are of course many other fly-fishing opportunities beyond fishing for trout. Among these are saltwater fly-fishing for species as diverse as flathead and bream in the estuaries, and deep sea game fish like tuna and marlin. On the freshwater scene there are several species that can be caught on trout tackle without the heavy specialised gear one needs to chase big game species on fly.

For sheer adventure and the romanticism of fishing, my favourite native species has always been the Australian bass. With a distribution from Maryborough in Queensland all the way south down the east coast to Gippsland in Victoria, this indigenous freshwater fish inhabits some of Australia's most beautiful river systems and is often subjected to heavy fishing pressure. It particularly suffers from the increasing degradation of our coastal streams caused by land clearing and the subsequent erosion which causes stream siltation.

Despite these problems bass are still about in reasonable numbers in the wild, and in recent times have attracted a great deal of attention from fishermen who are forming conservation groups and lobbying governments to install fish ladders, improve culverts and remove weirs in areas where such structures have cut off bass migrations to the saltwater to breed. Bass have also been stocked with considerable success in some of the large water supply dams in New South Wales and southern Queensland where enlightened water authorities have seen the potential for allowing recreational anglers to utilise and enjoy these resources with the added benefit of injecting much needed tourist dollars into surrounding local communities.

I believe the survival of any indigenous wildlife is well worth fighting for, and the old bronze battler is no exception. Ask any serious bass fisher and they will agree that there is something about this particular perch that really gets under your skin. Some would say it is the superb and quintessentially Australian bush environs they inhabit. Others delight in their aggressive nature and their no-nonsense approach to a well-presented lure or fly. I delight in the fact that they are a native fish and so perfectly adapted to their environment.

My earliest fishing adventures as a boy involved hiking through the wild country around the Colo River and into the upper reaches of

Wheeny Creek near Kurrajong, north-west of Sydney, with a backpack, a topographic map and an ultra-light spinning outfit. Serious exploration of those steep rocky eucalypt clad gullies revealed clear deep dark pools with deafening populations of cicadas. The fish had probably never seen a human being let alone the tiny floating lures my equally enthusiastic friends and I lobbed their way. The purity and remoteness of this environment and the gullibility of the fish made the whole experience quite intoxicating. It was certainly a substantial part of the great adventure that led me ultimately to trout fishing and then fly-fishing for trout.

Somewhere along the way I lost touch with bass fishing and only recently again tried catching bass on fly. What a shock to the system that was! All those years casting tiny flies to visible trout with the greatest care and delicacy went right out the window. Even intentionally plopping down a grasshopper pattern along the banks of the upper Murrumbidgee during the hopper season seems delicate when compared to the size of fly used to stir up the aggressive bass.

My friend David Brindley suggested we join South Coast bass expert Will Watt one evening at Berry and fish the famous Broughton Creek well upstream from its junction with the mighty Shoalhaven River. This was an opportunity too good to miss and we each caught several small bass and mysteriously missed about ten savage strikes each. David lost a big one—as always seems to happen to any fisherman—you know, the one that got away! We used large deer hair bodied floating flies called Dahlberg Divers. It was a bit nerve-racking casting these large air resistant flies as they need to be cast aggressively and sound like huge turbocharged mosquitoes as they scream back and forward past one's very nervous earlobe! The trick is to slap these monstrosities down beside any good looking undercut bank or sunken tree trunk and lower your rod at the last second to ensure the fly remains motionless and doesn't slide forward as this is a dead give away to a bass that has been attracted by the fly's initial landing. It is essential that you let the ripples subside completely, sometimes waiting as long as sixty seconds to simulate a creature that has fallen into the water and been stunned. Only then do you give the fly a jerk so it makes a chugging glooping sort of noise on the surface, and this often induces a bass to hit the fly with explosive force. Not a delicately sipping trout type rise, but a seriously aggressive strike with water flying and hopefully a hook up to a brawling bass. It is an unbelievably suspenseful and exciting experience.

You can't imagine anything less like fly-fishing for trout where finesse and presentation is often everything. This was a game of accuracy and aggression. It was possible with a considerable change of casting style to deliver these flies with some finesse but it was important to get the attention of the fish so the fly landing with a seductive plop was very important. We used our normal six and seven weight trout rods and floating lines with a shorter, fast taper nylon leader about nine foot long, and a large 1/0 Dahlberg Diver or a floating popper with strike inducing wobbly rubber legs. I had a great deal of fun with the Dahlberg Diver with its seductive rabbit fur strip tail. I wondered if the long tail was part of the problem I was having with hooking the fish so I trimmed it back to about two inches long and it still looked great on the retrieve.

Broughton Creek where we fished was a series of long, deep, dark mysterious pools with lots of sunken timber and weed beds. If ever there was a stretch of water that was picture book perfect for bass this was it. The creek was surrounded by dairy farms with cattle looking on inquisitively and plenty of large slushy cowpats to slip over in if you weren't careful. Having read and reread the early adventure filled writings of Harrison, Turnbull, Bethune and Starling over the years, and the way they so perfectly described the fabulous bass fishing terrain down the South Coast of New South Wales, it was a real treat to experience it first-hand. Will said the pools we fished held bass to at least two kilos. His young son had caught and released one that size just two weeks before our visit! I couldn't resist thinking to myself 'Hmmm, "you should have been here two weeks ago"— that sounds familiar'.

Of course fish of that size are prime female brood stock and something special, so we should all return these large females to breed for the future of bass fishing. Catch and release is the obvious choice in circumstances where natural recruitment and the genetic integrity of the fish in a river system are vitally important to the species survival. Keeping smaller fish for the table is perfectly reasonable but thinking fishers know that the big females should be released as quickly as possible to further enhance their chances of survival.

One particularly interesting part of the trip for me was the number of hits we all seemed to be getting without hooking up. The cast would be good and the action of the fly looked great. The bass were hitting aggressively but my hook up rate was only about one in four or five. When I caught up with Will and mentioned this he smiled and said that he had experienced the same thing many times in this creek. Several years ago he had decided to try and work out what was going on. With the help of polarised sunglasses and a good high viewing position, he found the fish in this creek would often hit the fly with their tail to stun it and if he left the fly still without striking they would usually take it a second time very confidently within a matter of seconds with a hook-up virtually guaranteed.

I thought he was pulling my leg, because anyone who fishes with Will knows that his leg pulling comes a close second to his ability with a fly rod! For me, this was a new concept, as I had never experienced this kind of behaviour in all my years fishing in the Hawkesbury and Colo Rivers or in delightful Wheeny Creek. I've never thought of bass as playful in the way that a killer whale will toss a seal around before finally killing and eating it. The bass I've caught always did one of two things: they followed the lure and then peeled off, or they just came from nowhere and hammered it!

With only an hour left before dark I decided to see if I could test this theory—not strike on the first hit and see if the fish thought it had stunned its prey. Would it do as Will said, and come back and take the fly a second time? I guess you know the answer already—I had some trouble not lifting my rod when they hit the fly, but when I managed not to strike, three out of five fish took the fly within a few seconds. One did not have a second go, and the other hooked up on the first strike. Hardly a big enough sample to be called a scientific experiment, but it was a good example of what a clever bit of angler observation can provide. It was certainly an interesting lesson for me, and something to store away in the old brain for another day or place when the fish are not hooking up on the first strike.

I'm so glad I rediscovered the old bronze battler with the help of my special friends in fly-fishing locally and from the South Coast. It was great to see a fishery alive and well. The Southern Highlands streams south of Sydney where I live once had substantial populations of bass but the building of Warragamba Dam to supply the water demands of Sydney stopped their essential downstream migration to spawn. As a consequence the bass population died out completely and apparently no one has seen fit to stock them above Warragamba in the Wollondilly and associated streams to recreate the splendid fishery of years gone by. From a practical viewpoint it would be an expensive exercise and when the fish matured they would migrate down into Warragamba Dam in early winter and who knows what would become of them. Without a fish ladder they would not be able to get to the brackish water they need to spawn successfully. As Warragamba is closed to the general public they would not be available for recreational fishing and without natural recruitment it would mean the government constantly having the expense of stocking the Wollondilly system with no guarantee of a return to recreational fishers upstream of the no access zone surrounding Warragamba.

Restocking the predatory Australian bass may well be a creative natural solution to the problem of exploding numbers of noxious filter feeding carp that are muddying and spoiling our waterways. To their credit, NSW Fisheries are already doing work in this area and experimenting with introducing bass into impoundments that are already infested with European carp. Fitzroy Falls Reservoir is one good example in the Southern Highlands and it will be interesting to see if the bass can wipe out future generations of carp in this waterway. They certainly won't bump off the enormous mature fish but the small ones may well provide an excellent food source.

Another good example of a created bass fishery is that in Lake Yarrunga, the body of water backed up in the Kangaroo and Shoalhaven River arms when Tallowa Dam was constructed on the upper Shoalhaven River. This is a tremendously attractive piece of water and fishing is allowed in non-powered craft year round. NSW Fisheries is also monitoring this impoundment and looking at the population of bass in the Kangaroo River as a result of the earlier stockings post-construction. There is now a fish lift installed on Tallowa Dam and this will hopefully resurrect one of the east coast's most famous fisheries by allowing several species of migratory fish to make their way up and down the Shoalhaven when nature dictates their annual migrations.

Bass on fly is certainly a fun filled experience. Floating around in a float tube or canoe on hot cicada-loud evenings anticipating smashing strikes on surface poppers certainly takes your mind off the difficulty of fishing for trout in summer around my neck of the woods. Don't put the fly gear away during the height of summer—get a few surface poppers and give the old bronzed battler a go—you won't regret it, and I guarantee you'll be the one hooked the first time one of these spectacular Australian natives nails your well presented popper.

Chapter 37

SECRET CREEK

Every fly-fisher deserves a secret creek. Not necessarily a place completely unknown to others, but a place you can get to know and feel a part of. A place that you can take a trusted friend and share together unselfishly, but still feel as though it is your own special place; an escape from the hurly-burly world in which we live. A place where time seems to stand still and old fashioned values still seem appropriate. These pieces of water are few and far between, but they can be found with a lot of perseverance and perspiration.

Sometimes a secret creek is anything but secret, and it requires a certain mindset to make it so. Claiming ownership of many of our famous streams is more an intellectual exercise than a physical one. Every fly-fisher dreams of owning their own private stream and being able to control what happens there. It is a nice dream, but well beyond the budget of most mere mortals. Ted Turner, the American billionaire, is reputedly the largest private landowner in America with hundreds of thousands of acres not only in North America but also in South America. One of his ranches in the north apparently has about eighty kilometres of one particular river. I think we would agree that such a stretch of private water in private ownership is hard to get your head around. Imagine owning such an incredible amount of water, let alone trying to fish it all in a lifetime. I guess in some ways the ownership of such a resource is something of a responsibility and an opportunity to go way beyond one's own selfish needs for privacy and indulgence of pristine fishing. Ted Turner is apparently spending a fortune on stream reclamation and making every endeavour to return this waterway to the pristine state it enjoyed prior to settlement, and the degradations brought about by over-grazing and putting commercial interests before those of natural preservation. Let's hope he is successful, and can find a way to unselfishly share such a precious asset with anglers from around the world.

In the southern parts of Argentina there are enormous cattle ranches called estancias where wealthy anglers go to catch enormous sea-run brown trout. The Rio Grande is a famous river that runs through some of these ranches and the fishing is generally only available to those fortunate few who can afford the breathtaking prices charged for a week of guided fishing in fly-fishers' heaven. While it is a dream for many of us to experience this sort of fishing, the reality is that most anglers need to be satisfied with adventures closer to home. This is where the secret creek comes into its own. A little time spent on favourite water can be very refreshing for the soul and more than adequate compensation for not always being able to make every wild fishing dream a reality.

I've had my share of secret creeks. Some were found easily and others were a real test of patience and perseverance. Some were easily accessible and others very remote. Some were able to be driven to while others required some serious walking. Almost without exception they have been small waters with tenuous seasons of feast and famine. Most of them are under siege with the droughts the eastern seaboard of Australia frequently has to endure. My favourite Monaro streams have been particularly affected for the past fifteen years or so, and one can only wonder at how our farming and grazing friends are faring economically in an area so important to Australian trout fishermen.

Classic high country rivers like the Maclaughlin River and Bobundara Creek often become completely dry in stretches. The Kydra and Kybean don't fare much better. One of my favourite secret spots was a back country section of the Numeralla River but this has been virtually dry for years. The good thing about these rivers is their ability to bounce back when times improve. With an active local acclimatisation society in the Monaro region and the assistance of NSW Fisheries, it is possible to get these streams back to their legendary status—we just need the rain. If ever there was a region of secret creeks and serious fly-fishing opportunities, the Monaro and Snowy Mountains must rank among the best in south-eastern Australia. Over the border in Victoria there are equally superb waters just waiting for replenishment by way of decent rains and the stocking of eager brown and rainbow trout fry and fingerlings.

To find your own slice of heaven it is often necessary to go to great lengths to research waterways, pore over topographic maps, read voraciously and make contact with like-minded locals. We have all heard about how shouting the local bar can provide some inside information, but a quiet approach to landowners can really pay dividends, particularly as fly-fishers are often viewed more favourably than bait-fishers or spin-fishermen. The idea of catch and release has come a long way; respect for the environment and particularly private property is almost always a winner with landowners who value their privacy and security. This is probably the best way of securing private access to largely unfished waters and that is what secret creeks are all about.

There are of course many tiny streams that provide fabulous fishing in public areas like the Kosciuszko National Park. This vast area has so many creeks that the potential seems almost limitless. Stop in at the Tourist Centre at Cooma and buy the 1:25,000 topographic maps that cover the area and you will see much more than a lifetime of fly-fishing opportunities, and a seemingly endless supply of potential small stream possibilities. The Eucumbene River is a perfect example that stretches way back into the high country and offers the adventurous angler the chance to investigate many kilometres of pristine waters as well as healthy little feeder streams and intriguing nooks and crannies.

The Thredbo River runs into Lake Jindabyne near the township of Jindabyne and is one of Australia's most famous and beautiful trout streams. It drains the snow melt from the mountains around the delightful ski resort of Thredbo. It is anything but secret, yet it has hidden stretches that see little fishing pressure, and that can provide unbelievable action in the warmer months. This is a stream that can really get you in, and allows a certain feeling of intimacy when fished for several years or more. There are certain times of the year when it seems like a piscatorial Pitt Street with what seems like every man in his wet waders tramping along its well worn paths. There are other times though were you can fish all day and not see another angler. This is especially true if you are prepared to walk a bit and explore some of the more remote sections away from the madding crowd. Granted, the Thredbo is not a secret creek by any stretch of the imagination or protected by vast areas of private land. It is mostly accessible by fit anglers and it can provide amazing fishing during the spawn run late in the season or early in the new season for recovering fish. It is probably at its best in early December or February and March for the dry fly enthusiast as the hatches are more regular and the hopper fishing can be a real blast after Christmas in a good season.

Many years ago a special fishing friend of mine, Bernie Stever and his wife Prue, had forty acres up near Oberon on the upper reaches of the Campbells River. This was his secret creek. We had some great fun on the brown trout up that way before the drought set in, sneaking around willow-choked pools and drifting nymphs suspended under buoyant dry flies like Stimulators and Royal Humpies. The trout loved them, and we learned all sorts of tricky ways to present the flies in such tight surrounds. Little drag-free downstream drifts and bow-and-arrow casts were often the order of the day. One particular day I was fishing a little Red Tag and was lost in the moment, when I realised it had sunk. Suddenly the leader moved and I lifted the rod to find I was connected to a feisty two pound brown. When I got her to the bank I couldn't believe my eyes. Her mouth was completely full of worms. Why she had decided to take my bedraggled, sunken Red Tag was a mystery with all those wriggly worms already in her throat. Perhaps she had disgorged them during the fight but no matter how you look at it, she was full of worms. Still I wasn't arguing at the time, I really enjoyed the battle and I released her to continue mopping up the drowned worms in that particular secret creek.

Another favourite creek that always comes to mind whenever the subject of hidden gems and special spots crops up is a little creek in the Crookwell region in the Southern Tablelands region of New South Wales. It is one of those spots that is hidden from the road by the local landscape and rarely fished. If you studied a topographic map of the area you would probably dismiss it as having too small a catchment and move onto more likely looking streams. It runs through rich basalt soil country and private property to join another well known stream that has suffered terribly in the recent drought. The secret of this little gem is that it is spring fed, and without this precious and seemingly constant supply of water it would surely be just a trickle that would never support the healthy browns and rainbows that it does year round.

I discovered this stream about fifteen years ago and spent many happy days exploring its potential and introducing it to several friends who also appreciated it for what it was. A delicate yet highly successful fishery that provided visual trout fishing as good as you could expect to get anywhere in New South Wales. In recent years it has been devastated by the dry times and has become choked with blackberries where the absentee hobby farmers have let it go wild. Hopefully in years to come we will see some serious rain in the region and this creek will recover after a decent flood to clean it out. The local authorities may insist the absentee farmers clear up the blackberries, but I doubt it, as they are as hidden as the stream itself. I know there are some deep holes where a few fish are surviving but in its current state it is virtually unfishable and has become just a happy memory for the time being.

Many years ago I had an unexpected experience while I was fishing for bass in Wheeny Creek, well upstream from where it runs into the famous Colo River north and west of Sydney. For years as a young guy I had hiked in and fished the upper reaches around Kurrajong and it was my first secret creek. As soon as I could drive I saved like fury and bought an old Volvo station wagon and then a much loved second-hand aluminium 15 foot Canadian canoe. My fishing horizons suddenly expanded exponentially. Spurred on by the evocative writings of Harrison and Bethune, I used to put the canoe in the back of the burnt orange Volvo and drive it into the Wheeny Creek valley along a track from the Colo end. How it survived that I'll never know, but that's another story. This was a particularly interesting stream because it ran through an isolated hidden valley that had been settled from the early days and at one stage had apparently supported about forty families and had a small school to educate the children of these market gardeners. They grew all sorts of vegetables and crops on the tiny river-flats hemmed in by the hard sandstone ridges, and barged them down Wheeny

Creek and then the Colo River to be packed onto boats to make the trip down the mighty Hawkesbury River to market.

This was real subsistence farming, and when I was a boy growing up in Kurrajong that little piece of history was long gone. There was no one living in the valley, and unless you really knew what to look for there was no obvious evidence of all that subsistence energy and physical occupation. There was the odd ruined rock wall foundation but no really tangible evidence of settlement. You could paddle for miles through what seemed like an untouched valley with virginal Australian bush hillsides that time had forgotten. The only sounds were those of nature, a raucous laugh from a kookaburra or those rude words that crows call. There were some serious bass in this narrow deep creek, lurking under the lily pads. Some of my earliest fly rod experiences involved canoeing upstream in the evening and catching bass on poppers. I slept in a swag or little tent and fished early in the morning before heading back to civilisation and a relieved mother by lunchtime.

One evening I was just paddling along with my younger brother Justin, further upstream than we had ever been, and we came to what looked like a castle wall on one side of the narrow valley. It was of course a sandstone ledge elevated above the creek, but it had a man-made look about it. We were so intrigued that I pulled the canoe up and we scrambled out onto the grassy verge and went for a look. As we walked along and looked up, it had for all the world, a feeling of a rustic wall from a medieval castle about ten metres high. We explored a little further along to where the wall became a small side valley and found a large sandstone overhang which looked like a side entrance to the 'castle'. Looking back now it seems kind of spooky, but at the time it was all rather adventurous. Justin and I squeezed in through the crack and found ourselves in a surprisingly large cave with a series of internal ledges. On those ledges were stacked all sorts of ancient camping equipment and boxes of tinned stores. We had stumbled onto a fisherman's secret stash. On the uppermost ledge was a stack of old bamboo poles about twelve feet long. They had lengths of nylon attached and small floats in a Ned Kelly style of rig. Just a length of nylon as long as the rod and a bobby cork type float with a single hook on a three foot trace. Below that were boxes of assorted old fishing gear and cooking equipment. There were four old camp chairs neatly stacked against the wall and tarps and other assorted stuff packed neatly by someone who had a very well organised mind.

Everything about the place was perfectly preserved. It was dry and obviously undisturbed. The tins had some rust on them and who knows what was inside. We were way upstream and had been so intrigued by the find, that we had let time slip away without really noticing. Suddenly the light was starting to fade and we had to be home that night. We had to drag ourselves away from what seemed like a perch fisherman's sacred site. As we hurriedly paddled downstream we vowed to go back and have another look, and try to work out who the owners may have been and try and date the equipment.

What with the history of the valley and the age of the stores it may have been originally used by someone who had passed away years ago and remained hidden and preserved until we stumbled on it years later. It is all a memory now as we never got back as we intended, but for the short time we were there we were intrigued by someone's secret camp site on their secret creek. It is a discovery I will cherish in my memory and never forget. Some of the finer details are a little hazy now, but I still occasionally find myself wondering if it is all still there, and who the capable fisherman was who stored all those essentials in that cave. How often did he go there and how many perch did he and perhaps his family pull from that secret creek? So many unanswered questions.

Looking back now I wish I had returned and found some of the answers. Still, it was his section of secret creek and his secret stash—perhaps we should respect that old perch fisherman and his personal possessions— and leave it at that.

Chapter 38

BUZZERS ON THE DEAD DRIFT

One of the deadliest methods I've found for catching trout in lakes involves using a floating line and a long leader with two small buzzer patterns attached. In competition fishing where three flies are allowed then the options can be further explored by adding a third fly in a different size or colour.

The Australian Fly-fishing Championships in 2004 on Lake Eucumbene were a perfect example of how this technique was utilised by the leading anglers and the results spoke for themselves. While some anglers struggled to catch anything from the boat in the three-hour competition sessions, other anglers caught four or five and lost several. This gave them a tremendous advantage in the rankings because it meant they won their sessions and put them in a great position to qualify for the Australian, World and Commonwealth teams. I had the good fortune to be fishing in my first boat session with well known Victorian angler Max Vereshaka. He won this session with five fish measured and he lost one as well!

The rig was pretty simple: a straight leader of at least five metres with a fly attached to the point and two more flies on twenty centimetre droppers at one and a half to two metre intervals up towards the fly line. This gives you a manageable rig that can be cast with a minimum of tangles and allows you to fish flies at three different levels to maximise the chance of finding the feeding level of the trout. The use of three flies was allowed by NSW Fisheries because of a special dispensation that allowed competitors at this event to use the same rigs that are allowed in most countries which host the World Fly Fishing Championships. In New South Wales we were until recently only allowed two flies and this is still an effective rig under the circumstances. With the recent change of rules to allow three flies we can effectively fish a larger part of the water column.

The best flies are small slimly tied black buzzers or red bloodworms on heavy size 12 to size 16 curved buzzer or straight nymph hooks, attached to fine fluorocarbon leader material to allow the flies to sink quickly as they drift in front of your boat.

The best locations were over creek lines at the top end of the bays around Buckenderra in about three to four metres of water. The takes were rarely subtle and the rainbows on this occasion fought like fury. The presence of substantial weed beds was an important factor and the trout were taken with the dead-drifted buzzers particularly when drifted across the breeze. The dead drift allows the flies to sink and then the action of the breeze on the floating fly line lifts the flies gently in the water column simulating insects heading up to the surface to emerge for their final act of mating and laying their eggs prior to dying—a deadly combination that invariably fools a feeding trout.

With this method, it is very important to keep in touch with your flies. This means not letting any slack into the line while at the same time allowing the flies to sink and then drift with the wind in front of the boat. A ten foot rod is handy in that it allows you to dibble the top fly in the surface before you lift off for your next cast and this lifting action combined with making the top fly twitch in the surface often gets a strike from a fish that has followed the flies up but not committed to them. This is a very subtle method that is equally effective from the bank in the same areas.

The English often use a strike indicator in the form of a piece of wool or another buoyant fly and call this 'fishing the bung'. This is also a method that is favoured in New Zealand where guides want to give anglers the best chance of catching some of the trophy trout they have in their magnificent lakes. One of the advantages often quoted by my New Zealand friends is that this technique minimises the chance of spooking the fish because there is a minimum of casting involved and the presentation is so natural. There is no question about its effectiveness as several of my friends and I have caught some serious brown and rainbow trout with this method.

Depending on the depth you want to achieve you may choose to tie your buzzer or nymph patterns on fine or heavy hooks. If getting down deep is important, then a bead head will often do the job and add a little flash to your flies. The simpler the fly is tied the better it seems to work. Black tying thread around the hook from the bend up to the eye and some dubbed rabbit fur behind the eye is a deadly buzzer, and a pheasant tail body and a little peacock herl behind the eye is also a simple and effective combination. For bloodworms which imitate midges an equally simple tie using red floss silk or flexible rubber ribbing in a transparent red colour does the trick.

I must admit that I'm an incorrigible upstream fly-fisher who loves delivering a dry upstream on as long a leader as I can manage during those warmer months of the year when the fish are looking up towards the surface for a delicate dun or a big fat cicada. Over the years however I have mellowed to a point where I now also enjoy deep upstream nymphing and across and down wet fly-fishing in New Zealand in fast running rivers like the Tongariro and Tauranga-Taupo that are open for part of their length over the winter months.

When it comes however to a method that is most likely to succeed in lakes or slow flowing rivers, the dead-drifted buzzer rig really takes some beating. It can be a very engrossing and demand a high level of concentration. It is a method that appears too easy but that requires finesse and an understanding of how best to represent this vital food form that makes up such a large percentage of the lake trout's diet. Why don't you give it a try next time you are fishing a lake? I think you will be both pleasantly surprised and richly rewarded.

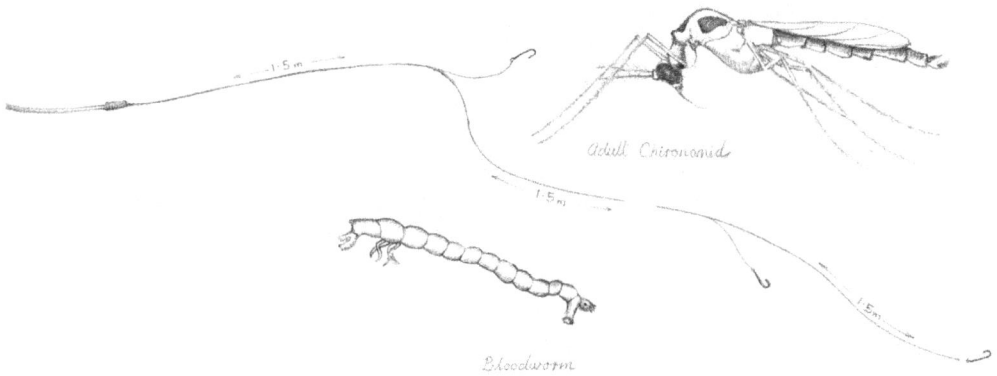

Adult Chironomid

Bloodworm

Chapter 39

THE ARMCHAIR ANGLER

Fly-fishing is a sport that can easily turn sensible human beings into unashamed gear freaks. You can find yourself at the complete mercy of tackle shop proprietors with all the latest 'must have' equipment you never realised you had to have.

Many years ago some bright spark came up with the idea of the float tube. This was basically a truck tyre inner tube with a sling in the middle to support the angler so they could float around in areas otherwise inaccessible from the shore. All that was needed was a pair of chest high waders to keep you dry, and swim fins for propulsion. The early tubes were pretty rudimentary but as time passed they became more and more sophisticated and large numbers of people realised they just had to have one.

I managed to resist the temptation for many years, as they were very awkward things to get into, and with fins over your wader boots they were hard to walk into and out of the water. When you did finally launch you floated well enough but your arms were barely out of the water and this made casting difficult. Serious float tubers found they 'needed' longer rods to compensate for the low casting position. If nothing else it was a great excuse to get another rod! Let's face it: 'need' is the fly-fishers most compelling four letter word!

The latest breed of float tubes finally got me. Now they are designed as a seat suspended between two pontoons that allow access as easy as sitting down in an armchair. Arm rests, back rest, spot for a drink or two and a fishing position above the water line means they are entirely practical and great fun as well. Two of my friends got them and in no time I was white-anted. They were off having adventures around the Southern Highlands in spots we had never been able to fish before and I realised I did need one of these craft just to keep up with the brothers Brindley.

Easily inflated and very portable, these craft can be carried over your shoulder into relatively inaccessible places then pumped up and away you go. The sitting position is very comfortable and you never feel as though you will slide out. There is no seat belt but a skirt clips across the pontoons and forms a platform over your knees. This feels reassuring and keeps your fly line from getting tangled between casts.

Propelling yourself with the fins means travelling backwards and this is easily accomplished and just requires a quick look over the shoulder occasionally. These craft offer marvellous manoeuvrability and incredibly quiet operation. The fish don't seem to mind them and are often caught up close. The big bonus is the wildlife you see as you drift silently along inaccessible shorelines. A fine example of this was a recent trip we made to the backed up waters of Lake Yarrunga created by the construction of Tallowa Dam in the Kangaroo Valley.

David, Mike and I launched at the picnic grounds near Bendeela Power Station and drifted along the steep and thickly vegetated shore flicking large flies close in under the overhanging vegetation. We were trying to tempt the Australian bass that have been successfully stocked in this impoundment by NSW Fisheries. The scenery was fabulous and the clouds were right down in the valley. It never stopped raining the whole time we were there and the fish must have been having a snooze.

We edged along silently and watched a variety of undisturbed wildlife including superb fairy wrens, kookaburras and an incredibly blue azure kingfisher going about his business. Stretched out on partially submerged logs were large lizards called water dragons or monitors. They seemed completely unfazed by these strange creatures sneaking up on them. We had to be careful not to put a fly too close as these lizards have lightning fast reflexes and have been known to launch themselves into the water and chase our offerings. They would doubtless be easy to catch but releasing one would be something of a challenge! By paddling very gently we could get to within a rod length of them and at that range the larger ones looked a little frightening. What with the tree ferns and dense wet foliage we could have imagined ourselves in Jurassic Park with the lizards looking at us impassively then suddenly diving into the water, and thankfully, swimming to shore.

We've also found these float tubes ideal for loch style fishing on smaller lakes and dams were you paddle upwind and then let yourself drift with the wind behind you just as you do with a drogue (sea anchor) in a boat. The fins are used to slow you down or change direction and the fishing can be fast and furious. Floating and fast sinking lines can be used in the same way as conventional loch style and its rather fun being towed around by the bigger specimens you often hook down deep on the lift as you retrieve the fly line and flies back up to the surface using this method.

When we use the term 'armchair angler' it usually refers to putting up your feet in a comfortable chair with a drink and a good book on fishing. It also conjures up images of open fires and wild weather outside. These new craft for armchairs anglers throw that old image out the window and open up a whole new world of opportunity in places you would never get to on foot or in other larger boats or canoes. They are suited to all ages of anglers as long as they are not pushed beyond their limits and should not be used in fast running rivers or snaggy waters where a punctured pontoon is a possibility. These float tubes are certainly an essential fishing accessory and ideally suited to anglers who appreciate the concept of 'need' and who like to do a little unselfish 'research' in inaccessible areas.

Chapter 40

THE ESTUARY ANGLER

Australia has long been known as a fisherman's paradise because we have such a vast coastline with an amazing diversity of fishing opportunities. From the tropics in the north to the cooler waters of the south we have an incredible range of fish species that can provide us with sport and excellent fare for the table.

These species can be caught from the rocks and beaches or from boats in our spectacular estuaries anywhere around our extensive coastline. Every available legal method is used to capture these fish, and in recent years there has been an explosion in interest by fly-fishers as they find they are able to catch more and more species on fly.

One of the classic places for fly-fishing in saltwater is the relatively shallow and protected water where our rivers meet the sea. These estuarine areas are havens for bread and butter fish like bream, whiting, flathead, mullet, trevally and Australian salmon. Up north there are even more exotic species like queenfish, tarpon, mangrove jack, barramundi…and the list goes on. All of these species can be caught on fly.

Many trout anglers are now branching out and trying their hand at saltwater fly-fishing and finding they enjoy it so much that they suddenly need an outfit specifically for saltwater. We've discussed before the fisherman's four letter word 'need' and if you want to become a serious swoffer as saltwater fly-fishers are called, then you do need a heavier rod and reel that are impervious to salt so that you can mix it with some of the more potent saltwater species.

Where the trout angler uses outfits in the four to six weight range, the swoffer can use these for the lighter species but will want a quality outfit rated around eight weight to ten weight and designed to withstand the tougher environment that saltwater imposes on fishing tackle. Coastal and estuarine angling often requires longer casts and more powerful rods with clear, slow sinking fly lines to match.

Good examples of estuaries and lakes close to the Southern Highlands are Lake Illawarra just south of Wollongong, and the mighty Shoalhaven River near Nowra. Both these venues offer excellent fishing opportunities from the shore or in small boats. Lake Illawarra is an enormous and largely shallow lake that supports vast areas of weed-beds and a wonderful population of classic saltwater species like bream, whiting and flathead. Picnic spots abound and it is a perfect location for a family day that includes some fishing. A scenic drive through Kangaroo Valley then down to the coast will see you crossing the Shoalhaven as you approach Nowra. This river is one of the most famous estuaries in New South Wales and offers the fly-fisher unlimited opportunities to fish for the species we've already discussed as well as Australian bass and the closely related and mysterious estuary perch.

To catch estuary fish we use larger flies because we need to impersonate the food they feed on. Prawns and small baitfish are simulated using flies with great names like Lefty's Deceiver, Clouser Minnow, Baited Breath, Pink Thing and my all time favourite, the Crazy Charlie. These are not delicate little trout flies but meaty beasts tied on hooks from size 4 upwards. Heavier rods and line are essential to cast these flies, as they can be quite heavy and bulky. The presentation of these flies is still important so as not to scare the fish but there is rarely the need for the sort of finesse in presenting the fly that we see in trout fishing.

It should be noted that any angler fishing our coastline or estuaries should take great care to protect themselves in this harsh environment from the sun with suitable clothing, sunscreen, broad-brimmed hat and polarised sunglasses. You should also wear suitable footwear when fishing from the rocks or wading around sand flats or areas where the bottom is made up of rocks or broken shells. There are some sea creatures like stonefish that can deliver a painful injury and foot protection avoids any such problems.

In a country like Australia where there are relatively few high cool areas that are suitable for stocking trout, it is hardly surprising that many fly-fishers have never been trout fishing. Our population is largely based in major cities around our coast and in most cases well away from the south-east corner of the continent where trout prosper. Nowadays it is increasingly likely that fly-fishers become swoffers first and may decide to try trout at a later stage. The old vision in many people's minds of the army colonel or elderly doctor in tweeds casting on a stream while puffing casually on a pipe is being replaced by a new generation in board shorts and sandals wading the sand flats.

These are exciting times for all fly-fishers and other anglers thinking of joining the rapidly growing swoffers community. Saltwater fly-fishing has certainly come of age. There is now a body of literature dealing with this sport worldwide and a handy Australian reference is that written by Peter Morse called *Saltwater Fly Fishing Fundamentals*. It is a really well written book that has a uniquely Australian flavour and answers all the questions one could reasonably ask about fly-fishing in saltwater.

When the weather is warm and the trout season quiet, why not pack a picnic and get down to the coast. Start with your trout gear and make sure you clean it carefully as soon as you get home. You may even find the need for an eight weight, then watch out—for the fun will have just begun.

Chapter 41

CREATING YOUR OWN FISHERY

Creating a fishery of your own is as much an act of selfishness as it is an act of generosity. Every serious fisherman dreams of owning a piece of private water, be it stream or pond, where they can stock their favourite fish species and enjoy the process of seeing the fish grow and the fishery develop. To be able to stock a private body of water for the enjoyment of family and friends is something that more and more people are doing as they realise the benefits and educational values that such an undertaking can provide.

One of the obvious ways to start a fishery is to stock farm dams and decorative lakes. This can be done with relative ease and all it takes is a call to NSW Fisheries or a visit to their website where there is some very useful information in the section on freshwater aquaculture regarding fish species and stocking rates.

In the Southern Highlands where I live, the most useful fish species are silver perch, Australian bass and in certain places brown and rainbow trout. From a fly-fisherman's point of view the trout and the bass are the most interesting species. Silver perch are very quick growing but as they mature they are largely vegetarian and therefore less likely to take a fly. Bass and trout on the other hand are much more likely to take a fly because they are predatory and carnivorous and this endears them to anyone who wants a fish that offers both good sport and excellent eating.

Trout require cool water all year round and this means a large dam that is deep enough to provide a cool sump of water through those few months of warm weather we experience in summer. Four to five metres are usually enough depth. Bass are less temperature sensitive but appreciate a waterway with some snags or cover to provide them with shelter. Neither bass nor trout will breed in farm dams as bass need to migrate to brackish water in winter and trout need clear cold running water over suitable beds of gravel in which to deposit their eggs in winter to successfully breed.

Rainbow trout generally grow much more quickly than browns and are usually easier to catch. Rainbows live for about five years and in a fertile dam will grow to a substantial size. Browns on the other hand can be a little more difficult to catch but live as long as thirteen years and will grow to an enormous size in suitable waterways. Both these trout will live together in the same waterway and in fact it seems possible to also have bass in the same dam. This makes for an interesting poly-culture with excellent all round fishing options.

The trouts are the more interesting of the fish mentioned in that they can often be seen rising to the surface to take insects whereas the bass are more inclined to stay deep and will only show themselves if there is a tremendous hatch of insects late in the evening on a hot summer night. Both these species give superb angling and they are all superb table fish.

For fish stocking to be successful it is necessary to look at factors like water quality and depth in any pond or lake being considered for stocking. Predators like cormorants can be a problem. We can get around predation to some extent by stocking with larger fish, or by slightly overstocking with fingerlings to allow for some predation and still see a reasonable number of fish grow on to become a worthwhile population for the recreational angler. Over time, as the pond is fished there needs to be further stocking to replace the fish that have been taken out. It is useful to keep records of fish caught so that they can be replaced regularly.

Brand new dams need to age a little to allow a food chain of microscopic organisms through to large insects to develop and provide a self sustaining food source for any introduced fish. There are ways of accelerating the ageing process by adding chopped straw and specific methods of fertilising the water. It is also wise to do sympathetic planting around and in the dam with trees that provide shade and look decorative. Water plants also provide cover for insects and fish and contribute to the oxygen cycle.

Some people augment their fish's food supply by feeding specially formulated pellets and this can be fun for showing friends or children the fish feeding and swirling around the surface of the dam. It is possible to train fish to feed at the same time every day by regularly scattering small amounts of fish food at the same place at the same time. This is also a way of making the fish easier to catch and some fly-fishers refer humorously to this form of berleying as a pellet hatch! Instead of the fish rising to natural flies emerging from the water, they are keyed in on the pellets and will usually grab any small fly that lands near them. While this would not be the done thing in the wild, it is certainly a good way to help children catch their first fish in a private waterway and start them off on the path to a lifetime of enjoyment and learning in the fascinating world of fly-fishing.

Chapter 42

FISHING DOWN
MEMORY LANE

One of the neatest and simplest pieces of equipment that a fly-fisherman can have is a fishing diary. Granted, it is nowhere near as sexy as a new high modulus graphite fly-fishing rod or an ultra-light wide arbor reel made from some alloy developed originally for the space exploration industry, but it is every bit as useful if kept accurately and faithfully.

A record of a day's fishing can provide valuable insights into what happened on that particular outing and what might happen on a similar day in the future. The time of year, the weather conditions, and particularly the time of day, temperature, air pressure and wind direction are important parts of the jigsaw puzzle. The moon phase is considered significant by some anglers and water levels and temperature can be vital to success. All of these things are interesting in themselves but become much more valuable when several years of observations have been documented.

Once you have a record to look back on it is possible to see some consistencies amongst all that information and suddenly patterns start to appear. Anglers who restrict themselves to a particular region and specific streams or lakes and fish them often, will find themselves building up an intimate profile of what conditions are the most suitable for catching trout in their particular area. They start to unlock some of the secrets that are largely unavailable to the bulk of anglers who just take pot luck and keep no record for future reference.

Equally important as the weather are details about what flies were used and which were the most effective. Any insects that were active at the time should be noted along with the flies used to successfully represent them. Sometimes trout can be incredibly selective about what they eat and this usually means they are keyed in on a particular insect and often a very exact imitation of both size and colour is needed to fool a fussy fish. On these occasions a diary entry explaining the subtle approach required that particular day can make all the difference in following seasons when the conditions are the same and the trout are playing hard to get.

Fishing diaries don't have to be purely factual or cold and calculating. They can include all sorts of fun and useful information. Many fly-fishers have an artistic bent and little illustrations just add to the flavour of any record of a day's fly-fishing. There are invariably funny incidents that occur

155

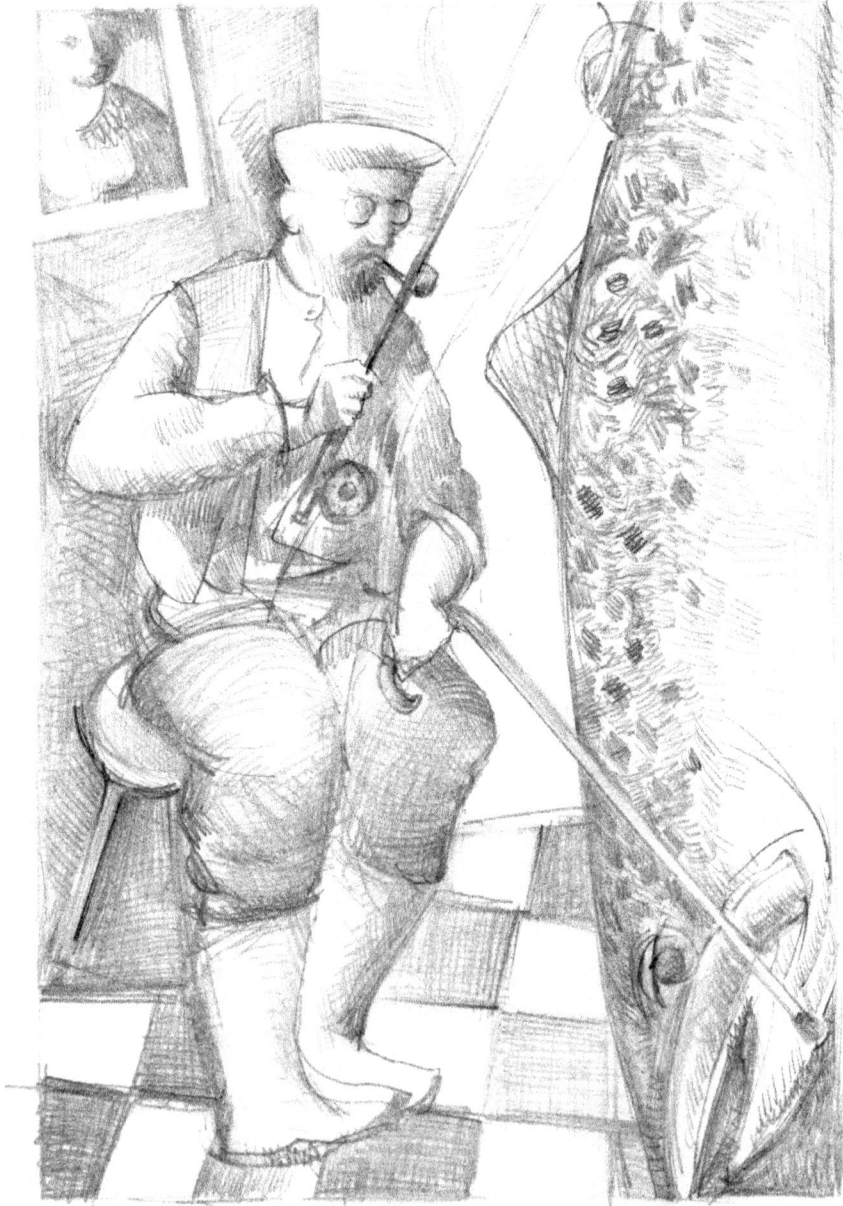

along a stream when two or more anglers fish together. A fishing diary can come alive with personal anecdotes and can be quite hilarious when read years later and related to the other angler involved. Especially as he or she may well have forgotten either genuinely or conveniently some of the day's events.

Who got to eat the first chocolate Wagon Wheel for catching and releasing the first fish was a tradition started by my friend Glen Preece, and needed to be noted when we fished together. I think Glen mostly got the first one; or who was able to stuff the most plump juicy blackberries into their mouth without laughing. I think that was me! Who was left hanging in the air by one arm above a deep hole when the branch he was standing on to spot the trout below suddenly gave way and crashed into the river scaring every trout in the vicinity and putting them down for nearly an hour? Who lost his balance and fell in on the last pool of the trip?...these are examples of the sort of valuable information that finds its way into my diary.

Sometimes we meet another angler and swap telephone numbers or nowadays email addresses. Sometimes it is a recipe for smoking trout or a particular knot that they find useful. Nature other than that relating to catching fish can get a mention. An azure blue kingfisher might put in an appearance, or my favourite streamside encounter of all, a sleek and buoyant platypus bobbing up and going about her business unaware of my presence. Those jet black eyes and quick slippery movements in the water and the ease with which she disappeared underwater as quickly and cleanly as she first appeared. Not only can that make your day but looking back on it through your diary entry can bring those memories flooding back. There is one platypus in a small dark pool in the Thredbo River that I have seen now five times out of six just before dark around Christmas time over a period of three years—very interesting and well worth recording. There was another platypus in the Kowmung River many years ago that I thought was a huge trout rising just before dark and I couldn't understand why it wasn't savaging my Royal Wulff until I realised what it was and had a good laugh at myself.

Collate enough of the more factual information and fly-fishers are often amazed at their ability to predict what insects will be about at any time of the year. All of a sudden they are catching more fish and making a dent on some of the mysteries we associate with fly-fishing. As the mysteries unfold it becomes possible to predict with reasonable accuracy whether a day will be good for fishing or whether we would be better to stay at home and mow the lawn or do something vaguely domestic to earn valuable brownie points from the other half to put towards future adventures.

A high pressure system on the evening weather report for the following day and a quick look at the diary confirms similar conditions from the same time last year. A call to a friend who lives by the river confirms the flow is just right and arrangements are made to meet at his place at first light. Last year your diary confirms that the best fishing was early in the cool of the morning and later in the afternoon as the air and water temperatures dropped. During the middle of the day the water looked great but the river seemed devoid of fish. Lunch was ham, salami and cheese sandwiches washed down with ginger beer cooled in the river. Your mate nearly stepped on a black snake sunning itself on a large flat rock by the stream and also got stuck in a most embarrassing way while crossing a barbed wire fence. He needed your help to extricate himself and swore you to secrecy (which in the case of writing this chapter just means not divulging his name!) There was an incredible hatch of snowflake caddis at about 6.30 pm and the trout went mad for about twenty minutes. You both caught two beautiful brown trout and lost one each in a frantic evening rise that only lasted about twenty minutes but seemed like an eternity. The successful fly was a size 12 White Wulff fished upstream and skated a little as it drifted past you along the current line between the fast and slow running water. The trout graciously took it for a skating caddis and you were frantically busy for those last few minutes of the day.

Facts and memories are at once intermingled and another day fishing is enjoyed then entered in the diary to add to the weight of knowledge gained from keeping a record of your fishing exploits over the years. The White Wulff worked again but not as well this time as your mates Snow Flake Caddis he tied the night before—he out-fished you two to one and the insect hatch didn't peter out until darkness descended and the temperature suddenly plummeted…

There are some great little diaries or fisherman's logs out there if you search around. I use a *Trout Fisherman's New Zealand Log Book* for my New Zealand fishing adventures which has eighteen pages that accommodate twelve day's fishing per double page. If you can limit yourself to one double page line then there are two hundred and sixteen fishing days that can be recorded and remembered at a later date. I've barely started mine so it will probably see me out as I only get to New Zealand for a week once or twice a year!

Of course a diary can be kept in a small notebook in your pocket. My friend Paul Greethead does this very effectively and can pull it out whenever needed and refer to an earlier trip and share with us the details of flies that succeeded or failed before. He somehow manages to keep it dry even though he is a fearless wader and goes in totally up to his neck on occasions, trying to get to the perfect spot or forcing his way upstream in some of the gnarly high country rivers in Australia and New Zealand. I think his secret is a zip-lock plastic sandwich bag. I'll bet the inventors of that clever little plastic bag with the resealable opening never thought it could double as a trout fisherman's diary protector, or for that matter, the larger ones are great for small digital cameras in a fly-fishing jacket pocket. I noted that somewhere in a diary years ago and followed up with a visit to the local supermarket and got a few. They have saved my fishing camera on several occasions when I've taken a wrong step and got a dunking.

Keeping a diary is for many anglers an impossible chore (particularly for us blokes!), but for those who persevere it is a constant source of enjoyment on a cold winter's night in front of a roaring fire. It allows you to remember the finer details of past adventures, and is of course an invaluable guide for the coming open season. It is also perfect when fishing with an old friend who has selective memory loss and is determined to live in denial about just how large his trophy trout really was—or how he left his clothes and fishing jacket hanging on the back of the door at home then raced out closing the door behind him and driving three hundred kilometres before realising—actually that was me! I just wish I'd seen my wife Julia chasing us down the road frantically waving her arms, but then we were just *tooooo* busy talking about those trout waiting for us in those high country streams.

Chapter 43

BETWEEN THE COVERS

For as long as I can remember I have been fascinated with books. I saved my pocket money and bought books on fishing because that was where my fascinations lay. I couldn't explain this early obsession but I was genuinely hungry for knowledge on freshwater fishing. I loved adventurous tales and I probably have every book my early hero Vic McCristal ever wrote about his Top End adventures in the Northern Territory and Queensland. They were exciting then and equally relevant now as I found when I went on a conservation hunting trip to the Northern Territory to thin out some very large feral pigs on a huge outback station south of Darwin. As I grew older I discovered John Bethune and John Turnbull. Way back in 1975 I was privileged to be the school captain of Richmond High School and with the School Captain's Prize (a book voucher for ten dollars) I 'invested' $9.95 in John Turnbull's *The Sportsfisherman's Bible* and have never looked back. It was here that I read the chapter by David Scholes entitled 'Trout Fishing in Tasmania' and the rot really set in! Those marlin and tuna and barramundi never had a chance. Something about trout fishing with a fly rod completely sucked me in.

I had spent my formative high school years trekking into remote sections of the Colo River and Wheeny Creek around Kurrajong north-west of Sydney chasing that old bronze battler, the Australian bass. The chapter on bass by John Bethune was completely credible as far as I was concerned because my youthful experiences bore out exactly what John was saying. The photographs in the book were superb for their time and must have made many readers plan their next trip as soon as they saw them. I know they had a very big effect on teenage me!

Only recently did I find on eBay a copy of John Turnbull's *A Fly on the Stream* published by Angus and Robertson in 1968. I entered the bidding war and secured it for a very fair price. It duly arrived and was in excellent condition with the original dust jacket in slightly worn condition—just worn enough to know that someone had enjoyed reading it several times as I now have. For the serious collector of trout fishing books a find like this is something of a triumph and a book to be treasured for many years to come.

Another author that had a profound effect on my view of the fishing world was Monaro grazier and angler, the late John Sautelle. His first book *Fishing for the Educated Trout* was a mainstay of the trout angling literature at the time. His views on tackle and camouflage were really interesting and his part in the acclimatisation work in the Monaro region of New South Wales was inspirational. I suspect he fished this region in the period when it was at its halcyon best. His stories of large brown trout in rich slow flowing streams and how to catch them on light tackle were highly educational. His fishing trips to New Zealand were brilliantly described and he can be held directly responsible for the investment I've made going there every year for at least the last twenty years! His other book *Champagne Fly Fishing* was written in his later years. It was a great expose of his tactics and attitudes as time had progressed and featured his younger friends Rob Sloane and Kaj Busch, as well as his son John who is an expert angler in his own right and who proudly carries on the family tradition.

It is said that fishing and particularly fly-fishing is the most written about sporting activity in the world and that says a great deal about the affection we anglers feel for our trout and salmon. I remember seeing an advertisement many years ago in an American *Fly Fishing* magazine for a company called The Anglers Art where they said they had over three thousand titles on fly-fishing—imagine that! It makes my four hundred or so books look pretty tame. Mike Spry, the legendary Khancoban guide and early fly-fishing educator, had a marvellous collection of nearly a thousand books. It is hard to explain the pleasure that a collection of books can give an angler. I know I can just stand and look at mine and feel a little overwhelmed at all the effort, love and passion that so many authors have put into creating their individual books, all of which make an important contribution to the base of knowledge available to anyone with the desire to learn more about fly-fishing in any of its multifaceted parts.

With the advent of saltwater fly-fishing we are now seeing a proliferation of books covering that part of the sport as well. Just Google the name Lefty Kreh and see what I mean. Old Lefty has been at the forefront of both fresh and saltwater fly-fishing all his life and what a satisfied man he must be looking back on his extraordinary life in fishing.

Getting closer to home again we have the late David Scholes who wrote prolifically about his fly-fishing experiences in his home state of Tasmania and other parts of the world. He was also a talented water colourist and pretty handy at pencil sketches. Here was a man that provided me with considerable inspiration and my only regret is that I never met him or wrote to thank him before he passed away. A little life lesson for me: don't procrastinate, get on and do it now. This is easy to say but harder to do, but invariably worth the effort. David Scholes wrote about twelve books and they all had interesting stories and lessons woven into the text. He was a very clever and passionate writer and one of Australia's most important contributors to the history of fly-fishing down under.

Another author from Tasmania whose books taught me an immense amount is Dr Rob Sloane. His *The Truth about Trout* and subsequent *More about Trout* are two excellent books on fly-fishing in Tasmania and around the world. Together with Malcolm Crosse he also produced *Australia's Best Trout Flies,* an excellent reference of flies and fly-tyers. These books are packed with information that will help the budding fly-fisher get a solid insight into the world of fly-fishing. Rob Sloane's father Tony also wrote *The Truth About Trout Flies,* a neat little book on effective flies and that is a worthy book for any keen angler's collection. Another book that Rob wrote, *Fly Fishing Fundamentals,* is an absolute must for any Australian angler aspiring to get a handle on the basics of fly-fishing. I cannot recommend it too highly. Its companion, *Saltwater Fly Fishing Fundamentals* by Peter Morse, is equally good for the aspiring saltwater fly-fisher.

Perhaps there is something in the Tasmanian water, because yet another prominent Tasmanian angler Greg French has made several important contributions to the literature on fly-fishing. Most recently his *Frog Call* and *Artificial* are both delightful reads that combine his love of fly-fishing, his attitudes to conservation and the importance of protecting the resource. He is also a master of conveying the importance of friendship in fly-fishing and in life.

For anyone interested in loch style fishing in Tasmanian or any other Australian waters there is *Essential Fly Fishing Techniques* by Neil Grose, a well known Tasmanian trout guide. This book looks closely at techniques that were developed in the world of competitive angling in the United Kingdom and brought here courtesy of the world of competition fly-fishing. I think this is the most comprehensive and intelligent coverage of these techniques I have ever seen. How great that an Australian author has made this important contribution to understanding all these important boat angling techniques that open up a completely new world of fly-fishing experiences for hardened upstream dry fly and nymph fishermen like me! In my copy Neil kindly wrote 'Paul – the Gods do not subtract from the allotted span of men's lives the hours spent in fishing...' A very nice thought indeed.

If only to prove the Tasmanian water theory, I would be remiss if I didn't mention Tony Ritchie's *Dry Fly-fishing for Trout,* Graeme Bourke's *Come Fly Fish with Me,* and Don Gilmour—the man who wrote the second ever book I bought on fly-fishing, *Trout Fishing in Australia.* This book, in combination with David Scholes' writings, really fired me up. Don's chapters on fishing for trout high up in the tussock plains of the Snowy Mountains above Adaminaby have seen me up that way on numerous occasions ever since, cursing the tussocks but loving the fishing.

Two other writers who emerged at about the same time as Rob Sloane was starting his excellent *FlyLife* magazine were Steve Starling and Kaj

Busch, a couple of real characters that are both able to convey the sights and sounds and feelings of fishing both in writing and on the Rex Hunt television programs. I particularly remember an article written by Kaj about fishing Lake Eucumbene, the massive Snowy Mountains impoundment in southern New South Wales, and how quickly the temperature can change there as evening sets in. He made the comment that you have to love the place because of how it feels to fish there and how you can experience four seasons in a day (my interpretation of his words) and I couldn't agree more.

Our friends in the state of Victoria haven't been backward in coming forward either with some superb writing in recent years by Philip Weigall who has now contributed six books including *Trout'n About, The River Behind The Hill, The Call of The River* and most recently *Fishing Season*. All of these books illustrate perfectly the man and his attraction to a life in fly-fishing. Phillip is one of the rare breed with the courage to devote his life to fly-fishing and guiding and writing about his adventures.

Rob Flower is another passionate Victorian who has made educational DVDs and written a really useful book *Australian Trout Food, Trout Flies and How to Fish Them*. Here Rob demonstrates his enormous knowledge of entomology and describes all the insects we anglers rely on when trying to fool our speckled friends. He lists a considerable number of useful flies based on his interpretations of the available insects and his knowledge gained from a very successful career in competitive fly-fishing and guiding.

Perhaps my favourite book by an Australian author is *Fur and Feather* by Peter Leuver. My first edition copy was one of my earliest purchases and a tremendous influence on my view of fly-fishing. This book encapsulates for me the joy of fly-fishing because it takes a number of flies we use in this country and tells a little of their history and gives a story of Peter's experiences using them in Australian conditions. Many of the places Peter fishes are coincidentally favourite little secret creeks of mine. Peter then cleverly illustrates the steps it takes to tie each fly and the result is a book that should be in every serious angler's library. No wonder it is in about its fifth edition! It is much more than a book about tying flies—it is one man's view of the whole picture and experience of fishing for trout. I recommend purchasing it to every new fly-fisher I meet.

For those interested in earlier Australian authors it is impossible to go past the writing of M.E McCausland in *Fly Fishing in Australia and New Zealand* and John Hedge's *Fly Fishing in New South Wales* and *Trout Fishing –A Season on Monaro*. These books are written a generation or two ago and are incredibly informative in terms of early history and techniques. Sir Hudson Fysh wrote *Round the Bend in the Stream* and described all sorts of angling adventures on the fly rod world-wide, as you might expect from the one time Chairman of QANTAS as he covered the

163

far flung corners of the world and obviously made the most of his position with our national carrier. He also wrote evocatively about his adventures in our Australian trout waters and there are some valuable insights which are equally relevant today as they were in his.

We only have to look to America to see a vast literature on fly-fishing. Who hasn't heard of John Gierach and his dozen or so splendid books with great titles packed with adventures on stream and lake. *Sex Death and Fly-fishing* was one of my earliest purchases and if you can't get away fishing, then a Gierach book is as close as you can get to experiencing the real thing. His adventures and friendships develop over time and his literary appeal is undiminished today. Moving more to the educational we bump into Dave Hughes who has written several really interesting books that are more instructional in their tone but equally as enjoyable as John Gierach. There are a significant number of American masters who have entertained and educated through their writings. I'm thinking of renowned publisher Nick Lyons of Lyons Press and John Merwin who wrote *The New North American Trout Fishing* which is an excellent read on the history and practical aspects of North American fly-fishing. Other luminaries like Gary Borger and the late Lee Wulff, Steve Raymond, Doug Swisher, Carl Richards, George Black and the voluptuous writings of English professor Ted Leeson and Datus Proper take us from the sublime to the almost ridiculous—and that's meant as a compliment. Several of these authors are what the Americans like to call wordsmiths. They are veritable masters of conveying a scene or a smell or any one of the thousands of experiences we encounter out fly-fishing, and they can do it in such a way that you can close your eyes and feel that you are right there experiencing the action with them. Now that is a gift. When I finally get over to the north-west coast of America and fish for steelhead it will be because of the pleasure I've had reading and plotting and scheming over Trey Combs' *Steelhead Fly Fishing* which is a classic on this extraordinary game fish and the masters of the fly who have devoted much of their lives to studying and capturing this migratory rainbow trout on steroids.

Great Britain has also produced some extraordinary angling literature from the quintessential *The Compleat Angler* by Isaac Walton to the more contemporary writings of Charles Jardine, Tom Saville, Charles Furzer, Peter Cockwill and the authors of that very interesting and insightful book *The Trout and the Fly* by Brian Clarke and John Goddard.

Looking a little farther back we find Frank Sawyer who invented Sawyer's Nymph, that simple little concoction that fools trout the world over. Frank Sawyer was a simple river-keeper whose modesty and simple lifestyle endeared him to all sorts of famous people including the legendary French angler and hotelier Charles Ritz. Frank Sawyer wrote two books on nymphing, *Keeper of the Stream* and *Nymphs and the Trout,* and they have been unbelievably influential to future generations of fly-fishers worldwide. Authors like Pat O'Reilly, Robin Armstrong, Chris Ogborne, Hugh Falkus and Simon Gawesworth have all made important contributions to technique, tackle and explanations of what the English call game fishing. The English and Scottish have devoted more books to salmon fishing than any other form of angling and the legend and lore built up around the capture of this prince of sporting fish has to be seen to be believed.

My main interest in the written word is devoted to living authors. I agree with the enthusiast who is a student of the earliest writings and appreciate that they are the well from where all other writings have sprung. Nevertheless I like contemporary authors or if you like the living poets of our sport. I have tremendous respect for the dead poets but prefer to collect books written from the 1950s up to the present day. It would take much more than a chapter or even a book to recognise every author in matters relating to fly-fishing. It would take a scholar a lifetime to read all the written material. I just know that I love reading about fishing as much as I do getting out there and doing it. I respect every author and while I might not agree with everything written I respect their right to their opinion and take gratefully what I can from the efforts they put into their writing. What more could an author ask—or an enthusiast reader offer?

Glen Preece

Chapter 44

THE AGES OF AN ANGLER

For the individual, there appears to be a natural progression through the world of fishing, an analogy of life itself if you like, where an angler's needs and aspirations change with time and experience.

Our earliest experiences with fishing are usually very basic and involve dangling a worm or prawn for any unsuspecting fish that might swim by: a harbour-side wharf or a quiet bit of freshwater in the company of your father or perhaps an older friend. For me as a little boy it was my grandfather on a wharf with a handline and a small piece of prawn. It's an introduction to the world of angling that either grabs you irrevocably with the first fish caught or sees you unimpressed and looking for other means of entertainment. A lifelong passion or something you might play at on your Christmas holidays.

One thing is certain: if you have the fisherman in you, the best is yet to come. Endless hours are spent reading and dreaming, and waiting for the next opportunity to get away and fish to your heart's content. Fishing magazines pile up by the bed, much to the delight of your better half. Fishing tackle shops become positively magnetic. They become impossible to walk past without popping your head in just to say hello. No amount of equipment ever seems enough, at least in those heady early days. There is simply always something else we need to make our kit complete, and if we don't actually need it, we certainly want it. This need is hard to explain to our partners but that's another story.

As experience grows there is the desire to catch lots of fish. Psychologists would have a field day right about now if we gave them the chance. There is something of the young man here with the need to prove oneself. Lots of fish, so hopefully lots of accolades. But time goes by, and the desire for lots of fish often becomes a desire for big fish. Suddenly numbers pale into insignificance when compared to size. One really good fish is worth any number of little ones.

There is a certain mystique with big fish. Something about catching a big fish says you've reached a new level of competence or piscatorial standing...or something. Hopefully at this stage the angler is now well aware of the precarious state of most of our fish stocks in the modern world. Catch and release becomes the way of perpetuating sport fishing for the future, at least in fisheries that rely on self-sustaining reproduction or natural recruitment.

Some fishermen never leave this big fish stage. Some just keep trying to catch bigger and bigger fish and continuing to prove whatever it is they are trying to prove. I guess that's how we end up with lists of world records, and for some people that is important, and an end in itself.

Other fishermen decide somewhere along the line that the degree of difficulty in catching the fish is as important as catching the big fish. The aim then seems to become a test of downsizing tackle while still catching large fish. Psychologists would be getting very excited about now if we let them. They would be revelling in the masochism of fishermen trying to make it harder for themselves to catch fewer bigger fish.

This is a particularly interesting phase and sometimes involves a desire for less fishing equipment but gear of higher quality. A heap of rods and reels are sacrificed in a garage sale or traded to finance a few seriously expensive outfits. This can easily be rationalised by saying that we need lighter or more responsive fly rods, and reels with more subtle drag systems to cope with the lighter lines and tippet materials that in turn enhance the challenges we are facing.

Somewhere in the mix, truly smitten trout fishermen often get a dose of 'oldtimesitis' and become fascinated with the tackle of times gone by. A good example is the fine old cane fly-fishing rods of yesteryear with deliciously soft whippy actions that remind us of the good old days; an era when gentlemen fished wearing ties and tweed jackets and smoked a pipe. These old gems are the handmade marvels of fly-fishing history. The sheer difficulty of their construction and the unbelievable skill of the master rod builder make you appreciate just how special these rods really are. Modern cane rods are arguably even better, but are breathtakingly expensive because of the labour costs in this modern world. Where a top quality graphite rod may cost a thousand dollars a new cane rod from a top maker can be three or four thousand dollars. You either need to be very wealthy or very committed to make an investment like this. About now the psychologists would be saying we should definitely be committed!

To gain this appreciation takes time and a great love for the sport. We find ourselves here a long way from numbers, size or meat fishing. Suddenly we've become sensitised to the subtle differences between purely practical tackle, and fishing with a work of art. The inexpensive modern tackle will get the job done very efficiently, and many anglers pride themselves on the results they get with cheap tackle, but when it comes to feel, response and angling ambience, there is nothing better than the best. In fishing, as in life, you only get what you pay for. Quality tackle can be a serious investment financially, but for the experienced angler who can feel and appreciate the difference, it is worth every dollar.

As time passes the really mature angler transcends the big fish stage and starts to smell the roses. Suddenly the experience of being there is more important. The mature angler finds the time to study his surrounds and take in a whole lot more of the scene—the big picture if you like. The need to rush or succeed or to prove a point becomes irrelevant. With age or experience, or more probably a combination of the two, we see an appreciative approach where the experience seems more profoundly important than the result. Just being there becomes the bonus.

It is at this stage that some of our best angling mentors appear, the teachers of the next generation, who are as happy instructing as they are actually fishing. Here we find the individual who has come full circle. He finds himself at the beginning again, enjoying the infectious enthusiasm of the next generation as he helps them on the road to the angling riches he has so thoroughly enjoyed. This unselfish approach is surely the pinnacle of any fisherman's career. Not numbers or size or whatever—just the opportunity to put something back into the sport we love.

Famous anglers over the years have thought long and hard about the relationship between a successful life and a successful fishing career. The idea that over time physical strength diminishes but is compensated for by knowledge and a growing appreciation of life's experiences ties in perfectly with the ages of an angler. I think the psychologists out there would like that philosophy.